RICHARD ROHR

The Universal Christ

HOW A FORGOTTEN REALITY CAN CHANGE
EVERYTHING WE SEE, HOPE FOR,
AND BELIEVE

Companion
Guide for Individuals

by

PATRICK BOLAND

CAC Publishing
Center for Action and Contemplation
cac.org

CAC PUBLISHING

Companion Guide for Individuals for *The Universal Christ:*
How a Forgotten Reality Can Change Everything We See, Hope For, and Believe

Copyright © 2020 Center for Action and Contemplation

Requests for information should be addressed to:

CAC Publishing, PO Box 12464, Albuquerque, New Mexico 87195

ISBN: 978-1-62305-052-8

Scripture citations are Richard Rohr's paraphrase except where noted.

Cover and Interior Design: Nelson Kane

First Printing 2020 / Printed in the United States of America

IN GRATITUDE

Richard Rohr's seminal book on the Universal Christ offers a level of clarity and credibility to a message very much needed to heal our world today. This Universal Christ Companion Guide for Individuals, based in the Center for Action and Contemplation's pedagogy, is a supportive tool for individuals to take this message into their hearts and live transformed lives. I am grateful that Patrick Boland, who has for many years been a student of Richard Rohr and the path of action and contemplation, agreed to undertake this work. Patrick, an Executive Coach and Psychotherapist at Conexus in Dublin, Ireland, poured his heart into this in-depth, well-crafted guide.

I also thank my colleague Vanessa Guerin, Director of Publications for the CAC, and her associate editor, Shirin McArthur, former CAC staff member and founder of Communication Clarified, who spent many hours editing this Companion Guide for Individuals.

We are all so grateful for the care Richard put into *The Universal Christ*. Through this Companion Guide for Individuals, I hope that the Universal Christ will be experienced more fully by each of you.

—Kirsten Oates
Managing Director of Program Design

CONTENTS

Introduction to the Companion Guide and Spiritual Exercises Overview

Welcome to this Companion Guide for Individuals for *The Universal Christ: How a Forgotten Reality Can Change Everything We See, Hope For, and Believe*, Fr. Richard Rohr's most important book to date.

The goal of this guide is to deepen your experience of the Universal Christ in your daily life. It is both a *meditation* on some of the important concepts in the book and an *invitation* to holistically experience a deepening connection with God.

Through engagement with this Companion Guide, you can:

- ▸ further reflect on how a forgotten teaching on Christ can impact everything you see, hope for, and believe;
- ▸ learn and engage in Christian contemplative practices that deepen this reflection; and
- ▸ set intentions for becoming a more loving, engaged presence in the world.

Although some of the questions are typical of study guides you might have used in the past, many of the questions seek to move us beyond focusing on our thoughts and reflections to a more holistic, embodied experience of the reality toward which Fr. Richard is pointing in this book.

Suggested Supplies to Fully Engage with This Companion Guide

- Journal and Pen
- Bell or Gong
- Timer
- Bible
- *The Universal Christ* book
- Companion Guide
- Candle

Journal and Pen
You will need a journal to record your thoughts and write down your responses to the various questions in the guide. This will serve as a way of recording your journey through *The Universal Christ* and this Companion Guide, helping you notice how both your experience and your understanding are deepening as you move through the book.

Bell or Gong and Timer
You will also need a prayer bell, or a digital prayer bell, to signify the start and the end of the contemplative sit exercises. Having an alarm clock or a digital countdown timer will help you to fully engage in the self-guided contemplative sits without having to check your watch/clock for the time remaining for each exercise.

Bible
Almost all the Bible verses are fully referenced in either the Companion Guide or *The Universal Christ* book. Three of the exercises, from the chapters entitled Before We Begin, 14, and 15, will ask you to read longer excerpts from biblical passages, so it will be important to have a Bible or Bible app available for this.

The Universal Christ Book and *Companion Guide for Individuals*
Each chapter of this Companion Guide corresponds with a chapter in

The Universal Christ. It is important to read each chapter of *The Universal Christ* prior to engaging with that chapter in the Companion Guide.

Candle

Depending on your preference and tradition, the simple act of lighting a candle or an incense stick might symbolize your entry into a focused time of conscious reflection. A lit candle can represent Christ as the Light of the World, which is of particular relevance to this book and Companion Guide.

Regular Routine and Timing

Developing a regular routine could be of help as you work through this Companion Guide. You may wish to consider:

- Choosing a particular place where you will engage in each chapter of the Companion Guide. This would ideally be somewhere quiet, where you will not be disturbed (for example, an oratory or chapel, a quiet coffee shop, a place in nature, or a room in your home where you feel most at ease). This place or space might be of important significance to you.

- Finding a regular time slot for working with this Companion Guide that you can schedule on a recurring basis.

- Determining how to begin each period of reflection (for example, turning off your phone, taking a moment of silence to "arrive," lighting a candle, journaling about how you are feeling, etc.).

- Determining how to end each time of reflection (for example, extinguishing the candle, journaling beyond the Companion Guide questions, praying in a way that is most familiar to you, etc.).

- Transitioning back to the rest of your day by engaging in a particular activity at the end of each session (for example, engaging in an act of service for someone else, going for a walk to relax, having breakfast/coffee/dinner to ease you back into your day, etc.).

Although your lifestyle may not always allow it, developing as regular a routine as possible will likely help you to commit to each chapter of this Companion Guide in the most personally meaningful way possible.

The amount of time you need to spend on each chapter of the Companion Guide will vary from person to person. A good rule of thumb is to not move on to the next question until you feel you have, at least to some extent, digested what you sense the question is about. Sometimes you may wish to go back and re-read sections of *The Universal Christ* before responding to a reflection question or engaging in an exercise such as a *Lectio* Practice. This will take additional time. I suggest that you re-read passages and go through the Companion Guide at your own pace. This will be more satisfying than "rushing" questions in an attempt to "complete" the Companion Guide.

What to Expect from This Companion Guide

- As this is an experiential Companion Guide, I particularly encourage you to engage in each of the contemplative sits and *Lectio* Practices. This is in keeping with the tone and message of *The Universal Christ*, where Fr. Richard outlines, in a variety of ways, that our Christ consciousness deepens as much from our approach to spirituality (experiential knowledge) as from our approach to theology (cognitive knowledge). Contemplative sits and *Lectio* Practices support this experiential knowledge by training our mind to be more aware of our experience and by opening our hearts to God's presence. There are detailed instructions for self-guided contemplative sit exercises as well as for *Lectio* Practices throughout the Companion Guide.

- There are quite a few questions for each chapter and several of these will take some time to complete. Rather than setting a strict time period for working with each chapter, I encourage you to go at your own pace, being present to the material and not rushing through any of the content.

- As you read through each question in this Companion Guide, take your time to read slowly and do not move on until some part of you has resonated with the quotations and the accompanying questions or instructions. The Companion Guide is not designed to be "completed" in a hurry. Instead, take the time to slowly read and re-read questions, or even full passages and chapters in the book, if you sense that this will be of benefit.

- You do not need to thoroughly complete this Companion Guide in order to digest Fr. Richard's book. However, if you do find yourself skipping questions, it might be interesting to notice if there is a pattern emerging in the theme or style of these questions.

- There is enough content here to last several weeks or even months of dedicated reflection, so moving from any mindset of "needing to complete" the Guide to "going with the process" will be most beneficial. Give yourself permission to take your time and read in a manner that is meaningful for you.

- *The Universal Christ* offers a worldview that Fr. Richard says has the potential to change "everything we see, hope for, and believe." A worldview this encompassing can take many years to digest and incorporate into everyday life. You may wish to return to this book on a yearly basis.

- The quotations and page numbers from *The Universal Christ* reflect the hardback version of the book.

Overview to Engaging in the Practices

Reflection
Most exercises in this Companion Guide take the form of a reflection. The hope is that these reflection questions will help you to process

the content of the book at a slower pace and a deeper level than if you were to simply read the book on its own.

The focus of each reflection exercise is twofold: to help you think through the concepts contained within *The Universal Christ* and to notice what you feel and experience as a result.

You will usually be presented with a quotation from *The Universal Christ* for the reflection exercise, but sometimes you will be asked to read a longer section from the book. At other times, you will be asked to read a passage from the Bible. After reading the passage, you will have one or more questions for reflection from that piece of text.

For example, in Chapter 1, you will be given a quotation to read on contemplation and then asked to "Describe in your journal your experience of this 'contemplative way' of learning." In the final chapter of the Companion Guide, based on Appendix II, you will be asked to "Read the following quotations and, going with your first reactions, journal what comes up for you."

Journaling

You might find it helpful to regularly journal as you journey through the book and Companion Guide. This is another, optional spiritual practice that can facilitate your meditation on the concepts in the book as well as help you to experience a deepening connection with God.

You might wish to create a journal entry for each of the reflection exercises in this Companion Guide. These can be single words or long entries, whatever feels most appropriate. Please note that this is only a suggestion; of greater importance is that you do not feel any pressure to "complete" journal entries, but feel free to process the reflections in whichever way(s) you find helpful.

Lectio Practice

Lectio Divina is a practice of reading, meditating on, and praying with Scripture. The Latin term *Lectio Divina* literally means a Divine Lesson. The practice originated where faith communities engaged in the sacred reading of biblical texts in the hope of receiving a divine lesson from God.

Lectio Divina can also be translated as "spiritual reading" or "sacred reading." These terms for *Lectio Divina* refer to the practice of reading other spiritual texts, as well as sacred Scripture, in this meditative and prayerful manner. (For a fuller description of the origin and evolution of *Lectio Divina* as a spiritual practice, please see Supplements I and II.)

Although some of the *Lectio Divina* exercises in this Companion Guide come directly from Scripture, most of the *Lectio Divina* texts come from *The Universal Christ*. As such, these *Lectio Divina* exercises are termed *Lectio* Practices, an umbrella term that includes both sacred Scripture and Fr. Richard's book.

There are four rounds of textual reading in each of the *Lectio* Practices in this guide. The four rounds follow a simple format:

1. With the first reading, allow yourself to *settle in* to the exercise and familiarize yourself with the words. Read the text out loud, very slowly and clearly. Pause for a breath or two before moving on.

It's important to read at an appropriate pace that sets the tone for your intention. Reading each round out loud will help you to identify the word or phrase that most speaks to you from the text.

Silent pauses are particularly important between each of the four rounds. In addition, the speed at which you read will affect your experience of these practices, so find a pace that resonates for you.

2. For the second reading, *listen* from a centered heart space and notice any word or phrase that stands out to you.

Between the first and second round of reading, you are encouraged to pause for long enough to really feel like you have settled into the text. This will enable a particular quality of listening, from a centered heart space, that will help you to connect with a particular word or phrase.

3. After a few moments of silence, read the text a third time, *reflecting* on how this word or phrase is connected to your current life experience. Take a minute to linger over this word or phrase, "to focus on it until it engages your body, your heart, your awareness of the physical [and unseen] world around you." (page 8)

    You may want to speak a response aloud or write something in your journal.

This is the round where you seek to uncover some of the reasons for the resonance you are experiencing with this word or phrase. Sometimes the connection is clear and you can easily understand the emotions and sensations you experience. At other times, your intuition or your subconscious will draw you to a particular word or phrase and you won't have a logical reason why it stood out for you.

The invitation is for you to reflect for a few moments, but not to over-analyze. Sometimes the word or phrase will return to you in the days and weeks ahead—and only then will you realize why it was meaningful for you. At other times, you will never make a clear connection with your life experience. It's during moments like these that Fr. Richard's notion of faith can be helpful to remember: "a calm and hopeful trust that God is inherent in all things, and that this whole thing is going somewhere good" (page 22).

4. For the final reading, *respond* with a prayer or expression of what you have experienced, inviting the infinite wisdom of God to support you in places of unknowing, confusion, desire, or hope.

    Allow the text to sink in and settle within your whole being before moving on.

Building on the previous rounds, this final reading focuses on expressing your response to the exercise. Sometimes you may feel hopeful or desirous of something and will want to make a request of God in prayer. At other times you might feel confused and unsure what the whole exercise was about. These can often be the most fruitful times of prayer and response. Your prayer may take the form of a written journal entry, a vocal prayer, or even a contemplative sit. Please choose a response that best suits you, and that encourages your connection with the Universal Christ.

Contemplative Sit

A contemplative sit is a spiritual discipline and a form of prayer with the aim being for you to be "drawn into more interior, meditative ways of experiencing God's presence"[1] in your life. It involves your remaining silent and open, in God's presence, to having your brain rewired "to think non-dually with compassion, kindness, and a lack of attachment to the ego's preferences."[2]

"Fr. Richard often says that contemplation is an exercise in failure."[3] This is because, each time we pray and despite "our best intentions to remain present to Presence, our habitual patterns of thinking and feeling interrupt and distract. Yet it is the desire that matters, and through our failing we encounter God's grace."[4]

1 James Finley, *Christian Meditation: Experiencing the Presence of God* (New York: HarperCollins, 2004), 24.
2 "Contemplation," *Center for Action and Contemplation*, https://cac.org/about-cac/contemplation/.
3 Ibid.
4 Ibid.

The contemplative sit exercises in this Companion Guide are designed to develop or deepen your practice of this form of prayerful openness to God and, as such, are very intentionally structured.

Contemplative sits appear in most chapters in the Companion Guide, along with detailed introductory instructions that can be read either silently or aloud, whichever you prefer.

Timing

The first sit, in Chapter 1, suggests beginning with a period of 5 minutes. This is to introduce complete beginners to this new practice of sitting in prayerful silence. For those who are more familiar with this meditative practice, I recommend engaging in a contemplative sit for a period of 20 or even 30 minutes. As the Companion Guide progresses, the recommended minimum time for each sit increases, moving to 10 minutes (beginning with Chapter 7) and finally to 15 minutes (from Chapter 13 onward). Please feel free to increase the amount of time for your sit to 20 minutes as soon as you feel ready.

Instructions for Each Sit

There are three different sets of instructions for the sits, all very closely linked and each with slightly different emphases. An example of the most frequent format (from Chapter 2) is as follows:

> Leading in with the quotation below, practice a contemplative sit. You may wish to set a timer or digital prayer bell for 5, 10, or 20 minutes, so that you know when to finish.
>
> Seat yourself in a quiet area. Once you are settled, read the passage aloud—this is the opening text for your sit:
>
> "To be loved by Jesus enlarges our heart capacity. To be loved by the Christ enlarges our *mental* capacity. We need both a Jesus and a Christ, in my opinion, to get the full picture. A truly trans-

formative God—for both the individual and history—needs to be experienced as both personal and universal. . . . *You are a child of God, and always will be, even when you don't believe it.*" (pages 36–37)

Reading

Each sit invites you to seat yourself in a quiet area, to settle down, and then to read a short excerpt from *The Universal Christ*. This excerpt is designed to focus your attention and allow an open-hearted engagement with God around what the excerpt seeks to communicate. Even if you read all the instructions in silence, reading this excerpt aloud can be helpful for grounding you in the moment and preparing you for the next steps of the sit.

There is no particular goal or emphasis as you read the excerpt; you do not have to focus on the theology of the concept, and you do not have to digest the excerpt in its entirety. Feel free to read it at face value, as it appears to you in the moment, or to read it in the style of a *Lectio* text, focusing on a word or phrase that stands out to you.

When you feel ready, move on to the next step.

Preparing the Body

There are many ways of preparing the body to engage in a contemplative sit. I have chosen a simple approach that is neither particularly strict nor technical. It will allow you to become aware of your body and, hopefully, to stay awake as you engage in the sit!

- ▸ Notice any tightness in your shoulders and neck and allow any tension in your muscles to relax.
- ▸ Allow your back to rest in an aligned, neutral position.
- ▸ Ground yourself and allow your breathing to settle.

We often carry stress and tension in our shoulders and neck so, by taking a moment to become conscious of this, you will be better able to let go of some tension as you relax into your sit.

The next instruction, regarding the alignment of your back, is simply to help with your posture, making sure that you are not going to injure yourself during the sit. Allowing your spine to rest in an aligned, neutral position can sometimes feel strange, showing how often we unconsciously let it curve it into an unnatural position. You do not have to sit bolt upright for the sit, but being conscious of maintaining a good posture will avoid injury and help you remain alert and present to any bodily sensations you may experience.

The phrase "ground yourself" has many possible interpretations and connotations. Here, it is an invitation to become aware of your presence on this earth, in this moment. You may want to focus your attention on your feet, finding a position for them that makes you feel connected or literally "grounded." Some people like to remove their shoes and socks, while others like to engage in an outdoor sit so they can feel the sand, grass, or soil beneath their feet. More than just grounding your feet, the invitation here is to become physically still and to notice the whole-body sensations you are experiencing.

It can be helpful to soften the focus of your eyes, allowing them settle on a point a couple of feet away from you, on the ground if you are outside or on the floor of the room. Alternatively, you may wish to close your eyes. This serves to quieten one of your five senses and help you focus your attention during the sit.

Place your hands on the top of your legs or knees, palms up or down, in the way that is most natural or meaningful for you.

Focusing

There are many approaches to focusing during a contemplative sit. Here are some suggestions of methods that you may find helpful.

At times you will find it difficult to focus as you begin your contemplative sit. You will be distracted by thoughts that seem to swirl endlessly through your mind. If this is the case, be patient with these thoughts, treating yourself with the same kindness and compassion with which God treats you. Then consciously choose to move the focus of your attention from your headspace down your body, first to your chest and then down to your stomach and navel, the center of your body. Imagine your thoughts and your egoic mind descending to the "grounded" center of your body.

Bring your attention to your breath, moving in and out, without changing your breathing in any way. Choose to focus your attention on this bodily sensation instead of the swirling, repetitive thoughts or attention-grabbing emotions you may be feeling.

Remember Fr. Richard's words in the introductory chapter:

> "*Contemplation is waiting patiently for the gaps to be filled in, and it does not insist on quick closure or easy answers.* It never rushes to judgment, and in fact avoids making quick judgments because judgments have more to do with egoic, personal control than with a loving search for truth." (page 8)

Take whatever time is necessary until you feel grounded and then move on to the next reading, which is designed to engage you in the contemplative heart space that is in keeping with the tone and language of *The Universal Christ*.

Then read the following aloud, pausing between each sentence:

——— "I am not trying to 'achieve' anything. There are no goals. I am simply becoming aware of this moment. Becoming aware of my presence in this moment. As I notice any distractions, thoughts, judgments, decisions, ideas that cross my mind, I let them go for now, focusing instead on my moment-by-moment experience of being present to What Is. God's Presence. The Larger Field. *En Cristo.*

——— "As I become distracted, frustrated, or confused, I consciously return to offering my moment-by-moment presence to God's Presence. God's Presence is already within me, whether I'm aware of it or not. No offering up is needed—I am offering in. Into the silence. Into each moment that I sit in contemplation.

——— *"'You are a child of God, and always will be, even when you don't believe it.'"* [Pause]

Based on some concepts from Chapter 3 of *The Universal Christ*, this text is designed to help you move out of being trapped in your thoughts to further enter into an embodied heart space. Ideally, it should be read aloud. It is important to pause where indicated, for a few seconds or more, whatever feels appropriate for you.

As you read through this script in successive contemplative sits, you may be drawn to certain phrases more than others, placing emphasis there as you read. This is perfectly fine. The manner of speaking this part of the script will help set the tone of your contemplative sit.

The final phrase you read will usually be a short excerpt from the introductory reading, a line that you may find helpful to hear before ringing the prayer bell to begin your sit. In this example, it is, *"You are a child of God, and always will be, even when you don't believe it."* Allow this line to "wash over" you and read it as a prayer or a benediction.

Toward the end of the Companion Guide, a much simpler contemplative sit script is used, based on a verse from Psalm 46:10: "Be still and know that I am God." By this point, you will have practiced enough contemplative sits that you are ready to begin with a slightly shorter introductory script.

Refocusing During the Sit

Don't be surprised if, at times, you lose focus as you seek to open yourself to experiencing God's moment-by-moment presence. During the sit, it is normal to be distracted, to feel bombarded by thoughts, to feel anxious or frustrated, or to want the sit to be over. This is all part of training your egoic mind to quieten. What is most important is how you respond once you become aware of this loss of focus and attention. Certain lines in the introductory script preempt this happening:

> As I become distracted, frustrated, or confused, I consciously return to offering my moment-by-moment presence to God's Presence. . . . No offering up is needed—I am offering in . . . into the silence . . . into each moment that I sit in contemplation.

The very first contemplative sit, in Chapter 1 of the Companion Guide, says that

> one approach is to try not to let your attention attach to any thoughts, feelings, or sensations that may arise. Allow thoughts, feelings, and sensations to arise, exist, and then fall away while you keep your attention open and large, connecting to that larger field.

James Finley comments on this phenomenon during a sit, writing:

> The guideline . . . is to be present, open, and awake, neither clinging to nor rejecting anything. This guideline applies to all the thoughts that arise in the mind. As each thought arises, simply be present, open, and awake to the thought as it arises. As the

thought endures, simply be present, open, and awake to the thought as it endures. And as the thought passes away, simply remain present, open, and awake to the thought as it passes away.[5]

In addition to this, some people find the use of a sacred word to be helpful.

Sacred words like Je-sus and Yah-Weh (spoken in the traditional Hebrew manner, with "Yah" on the in-breath and "Weh" on the out-breath, symbolizing the inextricable link between our very breath and the God who breathes life into us) have been used for centuries. The sacred word you choose is up to you, as long as it is personally meaningful and will help you to refocus your awareness any time you become distracted. Some teachers encourage the use of short sacred words that are no more than three syllables in length (e.g., love, stillness, gratitude) but others are more concerned with the personal significance of the word, rather than its length.

Several approaches to the method of using a sacred word (such as those of John Main, Laurence Freeman, Martin Laird, or the Jesus Prayer of the orthodox hesychast approach) involve the constant repetition of a sacred word, akin to a chant or a mantra. Other approaches (such as Centering Prayer) use a sacred word as a focal point to return your attention to a position of openness and rest, ready to re-engage in the moment-by-moment experience of God's Presence.[6]

If you prefer, rather than repeating a sacred word during the contemplative sits in this Companion Guide, you can simply focus on your breath—in and out—whenever distracting thoughts cross your mind.

5 Finley, *Christian Meditation*, 26.
6 Thomas Keating, "The Difference Between Centering Prayer and Dom John Main's Christian Meditation," *Contemplative Outreach*, November 2017, https://www.contemplativeoutreach.org/article/difference-between-centering-prayer-and-dom-john-mains-christian-meditation.

Again, this is an aid in bringing your attention back to the present moment. This approach, of returning to your breath, is the method given as part of the instructions for each sit.

Finishing Your Sit

The final instruction, after the closing bell has sounded, is to take some moments to process anything that may have come up for you during the sit. There is no obligation to do this, but journaling your experiences—from bodily sensations to thoughts and emotions—can be helpful to review as you come to the end of the Companion Guide.

The practice of a contemplative sit is just one of many spiritual disciplines included in the Companion Guide to aid your deepening connection with the Universal Christ in your daily life.

Staying within Your Comfort Zone

If any aspect of the self-guided instructions throughout this Companion Guide are unhelpful or off-putting for you, please feel completely free to change the approach to suit your needs. There are many people that have unhealed pain or trauma in their lives that might be triggered by certain body postures, breathing techniques, or imagination exercises, so it will be important for you to adapt those instructions to your particular circumstances.

This pain or trauma could be from a childhood experience or more recent events. It might be something of which you are fully aware or it might be hidden in your body. As you enter into a contemplative practice that brings you into your body, the pain or trauma can unexpectedly arise and cause overwhelming sensations. For example, you might start an exercise and begin to experience very negative emotions or sensations (such as dizziness, rage, intense crying, hyperventilation, or disconnection from your body).

Of most importance, as you work your way through this Companion Guide, is that you do not push yourself beyond your comfort zone. If you find that you are regularly experiencing overwhelming emotions or physical sensations, I recommend that you stop using the Companion Guide and discuss these experiences with a mental health professional (e.g., a counsellor, psychotherapist, or psychiatrist). However, if you have the capacity to work with what is arising, below are some adaptations and interventions you could try.

During the practice:

- Stop focusing your attention on your breath and choose to focus on what you can hear or see.
- Keep our eyes open.
- Change the position of your body during the practice (e.g., stand up, lie down, walk).
- Find a different room or place to practice.
- Choose a new sacred word.
- Instead of choosing a word, use one or more of your five senses to refocus your attention.
- Hold something with you that makes you feel safe and "at home" when you touch it (e.g., a piece of fabric or a small keepsake).
- Shorten the time of your practice.

If you feel unexpectedly triggered, please consider supporting yourself in the following ways:

- Simply stop the contemplative sit or other spiritual practice.
- Speak aloud to yourself (e.g., "It's ok, I'm ok. I am here now and safe in this moment, not trapped in a past experience that wasn't so safe.").
- Stand up and walk around.

- Touch the floor, the ground, or something with you that makes you feel safe and "at home" when you touch it (e.g., a piece of fabric or a small keepsake).

- Smell something that brings good memories to mind (e.g., a favorite food, fragrance, or essential oil).

- Listen to a piece of music or any sound that brings you a sense of calm.

- Look at a photo of someone or something that has very good memories or connotations for you.

- In the absence of a photo, picture in your mind's eye an image with good memories or connotations or say it aloud (e.g., "The warm sun, the blue sea").

Again, as you work your way through this Companion Guide, do not push yourself beyond your comfort zone. Our hope is that you will feel very safe as you deepen your spiritual practice throughout this Companion Guide.

REFLECTIONS

Before We Begin

1. Reflection

> "You must allow some of the words in this book *to remain partially mysterious, at least for a while*. I know this can be dissatisfying and unsettling to our egoic mind, which wants to be in control every step of the way. Yet this is precisely that contemplative way of reading and listening, and thus being drawn forward into a much Larger Field." (page 6)

Choose a passage or an idea from this chapter that does not make complete sense to you. Read it over a few times, making sure that it is still a bit of an enigma (if it begins to make sense, then choose another passage that is *"partially mysterious"* to you right now).

- ▸ What is it like to not "be in control every step of the way"? Notice any emotions or sensations that you feel in your body.

- ▸ Describe in your journal your experience of this "contemplative way" of learning.

2. Reflection

> "The revelation of the Risen Christ as ubiquitous and eternal was clearly affirmed in the Scriptures (Colossians 1, Ephesians 1, John 1, Hebrews 1) and in the early church, when the euphoria of the Christian faith was still creative and expanding. In our time, however, this deep mode of seeing must be approached as something of a reclamation project. When the Western church separated from the East in the Great Schism of 1054, we gradually lost this profound understanding of how God has been liberating and loving all that is. Instead, we gradually limited the Divine Presence to the single body of Jesus, *when perhaps it is as ubiquitous as light itself—and uncircumscribable by human boundaries.*" (page 4)

Take some time to read at least one of the four New Testament chapters mentioned in the quote above.

- ▸ From the passage you have just read, in what ways is "the revelation of the Risen Christ" understood to be "ubiquitous and eternal"?
- ▸ How does this idea compare with what you have been taught and have previously understood the Divine Presence to mean?

3. Reflection

> "The mystic sees things in their wholeness, their connection, their universal and divine frame. . . . Mystics get the whole *gestalt* in one picture, as it were, and thus they often bypass our more sequential and separated way of seeing the moment. In this, they tend to be closer to poets and artists than to linear thinkers." (page 1)

- ▸ From your own life experience, how can you relate to this understanding of a mystic?

- Take a few moments to return to the Scripture passage you just read (from the previous reflection) and read it once more, this time from the perspective of a mystic. Notice if this perspective changes your reading or understanding of the text. You may wish to note down any insights in your journal.

4. Reflection

> "*Your religion is not the church you belong to, but the cosmos you live inside of.* Once we know that the entire physical world around us, all of creation, is both the hiding place and the revelation place for God, this world becomes home, safe, enchanted, offering grace to any who look deeply. I call that kind of deep and calm seeing 'contemplation.' . . . *Contemplation is waiting patiently for the gaps to be filled in, and it does not insist on quick closure or easy answers . . .* [rather] a loving search for truth." (pages 6–8)

- As you read this quotation, which word or phrase most resonated with you?
- Repeat the word or phrase out loud a couple of times.
- Now take a minute of silence to reflect on the same word or phrase, allowing it to "wash over" you. Notice what emotions, sensations, and/or thoughts arise within you during this time of silent reflection.
- When you feel ready, write down a sentence or two that reflects this experience. You might write about the emotions or the sensations that you experienced and/or the thoughts that arose that were related to the word or phrase.
- Take a moment to read over your notes a couple of times. Feel free to add a sentence or two.

Take your time and only move on when it feels like this exercise has been completed.

5. Reflection

> "*Christ is everywhere.*
> *In Him every kind of life has a meaning and a solid connection.*
> I intend these pauses in the text as invitations for you to linger with an idea, to focus on it until it engages your body, your heart, your awareness of the physical world around you, and most especially your core connection with a larger field." (page 8)

Taking up Fr. Richard's invitation, linger with the phrase "*Christ is everywhere.*"

- ▸ After a few minutes of lingering, write down a line or two about your awareness of "your core connection with a larger field."

6. Nature Exercise

> "If my own experience is any indication, the message in this book can transform the way you see and the way you live in your everyday world. It can offer you the deep and universal meaning that Western civilization seems to lack and long for today. It has the potential to reground Christianity as a natural religion and not one simply based on a special revelation, available only to a few lucky enlightened people." (page 6)

- ▸ What is your experience of "Christianity [being] a natural religion and not one simply based on a special revelation, available only to a few lucky enlightened people"?

Sit with the following quotation for a minute, perhaps repeating it out loud a few times:

> "*Christ is everywhere.*
> *In Him every kind of life has a meaning and a solid connection.*"

- ▸ Now go for a walk in nature. Look up at the sky, go outside and breathe in the air, gaze at a plant, pet an animal, or simply pick up a stone. Can you sense the life in the natural world around you? Take as much time as you need, until you experience a solid connection between yourself and something in the natural world.
- ▸ You may wish to note down any insights in your journal.

7. Reflection

> "Truly enlightened people see oneness because they *look out from oneness*, instead of labeling everything as superior and inferior, in or out. If you think you are *privately* 'saved' or enlightened, then you are neither saved nor enlightened, it seems to me!" (page 7)

- ▸ What do you think of this idea of seeing oneness in the world?
- ▸ Reflecting on your family, your work colleagues, your friendships, or your local community, what would it be like to move away from seeing people as "in or out," "superior [or] inferior," and toward including "everyone and everything"?

8. *Lectio* Practice

After reading the following instructions, slowly read aloud the quotation below four times, following these instructions.

1.   With the first reading, allow yourself to *settle in* to the exercise and familiarize yourself with the words. Read the text out loud, very slowly and clearly. Pause for a breath or two before moving on.

2.   For the second reading, *listen* from a centered heart space and notice any word or phrase that stands out to you.

3.   After a few moments of silence, read the text a third time, *reflecting* on how this word or phrase is connected to your current life experience. Take a minute to linger over this word or phrase, "to focus on it until it engages your body, your heart, your awareness of the physical [and unseen] world around you." (page 8)

      You may want to speak a response aloud or write something in your journal.

4.   For the final reading, *respond* with a prayer or expression of what you have experienced, inviting the infinite wisdom of God to support you in places of unknowing, confusion, desire, or hope.

      "A cosmic notion of the Christ competes with and excludes no one, but includes everyone and everything (Acts 10:15, 34) and allows Jesus Christ to finally be a God figure worthy of the entire universe." (page 7)

ONE

Christ Is Not Jesus's Last Name

1. Reflection

Remember:

> "You must allow some of the words in this book *to remain partially mysterious, at least for a while*. I know this can be dissatisfying and unsettling to our egoic mind, which wants to be in control every step of the way. Yet this is precisely that contemplative way of reading and listening, and thus being drawn forward into a much Larger Field." (page 6)

Read the following quotes:

> "*Christ is God, and Jesus is the Christ's historical manifestation in time.*" (page 19)

> "The evolving, universe-spinning Christ Mystery, in which all of us take part, is the subject of this book. Jesus is a map for the time-bound and personal level of life, and Christ is the blueprint for all time and space and life itself." (page 20)

Notice how you feel as your read these quotes.

- ► What images and ideas arise for you when you read the words "Jesus" and "Christ"?
- ► Are there particular images and ideas about the words "Jesus" and "Christ" that are being challenged? You may want to record these reflections in your journal.

2. Reflection

Read the following quotations from Chapter 1. Notice what you resist and what resonates with you.

> "*Everything visible, without exception, is the outpouring of God.* What else could it really be? 'Christ' is a word for the Primordial Template ('*Logos*') through whom 'all things came into being, and not one *thing* had its being except through him' (John 1:3)." (page 13)

> "I want to suggest that the first incarnation was the moment described in Genesis 1, when God joined in unity with the physical universe and became the light inside of everything. (This, I believe, is why *light* is the subject of the first day of creation, and its speed is now recognized as the one universal constant.) The incarnation, then, is not only 'God becoming Jesus.' It is a much broader event, which is why John first describes God's presence in the general word 'flesh' (John 1:14) . . . the Christ that the rest of us continue to encounter in other human beings, a mountain, a blade of grass, or a starling." (page 13)

- ► Record any reflections you might have in your journal.

3. Reflection

Slowly read over this quotation two or three times, then ponder the questions below.

> "The Christ Mystery is the New Testament's attempt to name this visibility or *see-ability* that occurred on the first day. Remember, *light is not so much what you directly see as that by which you see everything else.* . . . Scientists have discovered that what looks like darkness to the human eye is actually filled with tiny particles called 'neutrinos,' slivers of light that pass through the entire universe. Apparently there is no such thing as total darkness anywhere, even though the human eye thinks there is. John's Gospel was more accurate than we realized when it described Christ as 'a light that darkness cannot overcome' (1:5)." (page 14)

Darkness
"Apparently there is no such thing as total darkness anywhere, even though the human eye thinks there is." What connotations arise when you read the word "darkness" in this quote? (You may wish to say it aloud a few times to feel its full effect.)

Pay attention to any physical sensations in your body and any emotions that you feel. What is evoked?

Light
Reflecting on your daily life, how bright is the light "by which you see everything else"? Who or what is influencing that perception?

Silence
To finish, take a couple of minutes to silently reflect on the following:

> "There is no such thing as total darkness anywhere."
> "Christ as 'a light that darkness cannot overcome.'"

4. Reflection

> "But instead of saying that God came *into* the world through Jesus, maybe it would be better to say that Jesus came *out of* an already Christ-soaked world. . . . When I know that the world around me is both the hiding place and the revelation of God, I can no longer make a significant distinction between the natural and the supernatural, between the holy and the profane. (A divine 'voice' makes this exactly clear to a very resistant Peter in Acts 10.) Everything I see and know is indeed one *'uni-verse,'* revolving around one coherent center." (page 15)

Spend a few moments reflecting on the notion that "Jesus came *out of* an already Christ-soaked world."

Trusting your intuition and resisting any temptation to edit yourself, journal any images and ideas that come up for you.

5. *Lectio* Practice

Introductory quote:

> "Ironically, millions of the very devout who are waiting for the 'Second Coming' have largely missed the first [creation]—and the third [ongoing beloved community]! I'll say it again: *God loves things by becoming them.* . . . God did so in the creation of the universe and of Jesus, and continues to do so in the ongoing human Body of Christ (1 Corinthians 12:12ff.)." (page 20)

The text for this *Lectio* Practice is:

> *"God loves things by becoming them."*

1. With the first reading, allow yourself to *settle in* to the exercise and familiarize yourself with the words. Read the text out loud, very slowly and clearly. Pause for a breath or two before moving on.

2. For the second reading, *listen* from a centered heart space and notice any word or phrase that stands out to you.

3. After a few moments of silence, read the text a third time, *reflecting* on how this word or phrase is connected to your current life experience. Take a minute to linger over this word or phrase, "to focus on it until it engages your body, your heart, your awareness of the physical [and unseen] world around you." (page 8)

   You may want to speak a response aloud or write something in your journal.

4. For the final reading, *respond* with a prayer or expression of what you have experienced and how you might feel drawn to pray to a God that "loves things by becoming them."

6. Reflection

"It is impossible to make individuals feel sacred inside of a profane, empty, or accidental universe. This way of seeing makes us feel separate and competitive, striving to be superior instead of deeply connected, seeking ever-larger circles of union." (page 16)

"Our faith became a competitive theology with various parochial theories of salvation, instead of a universal cosmology inside of which all can live with an inherent dignity. Right now, perhaps more than ever, we need a God as big as the still-expanding universe, or educated people will continue to think of God as a mere add-on to a world

that is already awesome, beautiful, and worthy of praise in itself. If Jesus is not also presented as Christ, I predict more and more people will not so much actively rebel against Christianity as just gradually lose interest in it." (page 17)

- ▸ What is your experience of Christianity being "a competitive theology" in which people are gradually losing interest?
- ▸ Where might this kind of faith be inhibiting people's ability to "live with an inherent dignity"?

7. Reflection

"What I am calling in this book an *incarnational worldview* is the profound recognition of the presence of the divine in literally 'every thing' and 'every one.' It is the key to mental and spiritual health, as well as to a kind of basic contentment and happiness. An incarnational worldview is the only way we can reconcile our inner worlds with the outer one, unity with diversity, physical with spiritual, individual with corporate, and divine with human." (page 18)

"But if you believe Jesus's main purpose is to provide a means of personal, individual salvation, it is all too easy to think that he doesn't have anything to do with human history—with war or injustice, or destruction of nature, or anything that contradicts our egos' desires or our cultural biases. *We ended up spreading our national cultures under the rubric of Jesus, instead of a universally liberating message under the name of Christ.*" (page 18)

- ▸ In what ways have your own life experiences reflected "*a universally liberating message*" and "an *incarnational worldview*"?
- ▸ In your own words, write down *your* version of the "*universally liberating message*" of Christianity.

Notice any temptation to edit yourself or to write down "the right answer." Instead, trust your instinct and connect with whatever *you* have experienced as liberating. Nobody else needs to read this.

8. Reflection

"Unfortunately, the notion of faith that emerged in the West was much more *a rational assent to the truth of certain mental beliefs, rather than a calm and hopeful trust that God is inherent in all things, and that this whole thing is going somewhere good.* Predictably, we soon separated intellectual belief (which tends to differentiate and limit) from love and hope (which unite and thus eternalize). As Paul says in his great hymn to love, 'There are only three things that last, faith, hope and love' (1 Corinthians 13:13). All else passes.

Faith, hope, and love are the very nature of God, and thus the nature of all Being.

Such goodness cannot die. (Which is what we mean when we say 'heaven.')" (page 22)

- ▸ In what ways are you skeptical that "*this whole thing is going somewhere good*"?
- ▸ In the coming days, notice where faith, hope, and love exist in you. What brings them to your attention?

9. Contemplative Sit

Leading in with the quotation below, practice a contemplative sit. You may wish to set a timer or digital prayer bell for 5, 10, or 20 minutes, so that you know when to finish. If engaging in a contemplative sit is new to you, begin with 5 minutes.

- Seat yourself in a quiet area.
- Ground yourself and allow your breathing to settle.
- Notice any tightness in your shoulders and neck and allow any tension in your muscles to relax.
- Allow your back to rest in an aligned, neutral position.
- Once you are settled, read the following passage aloud—this is the opening text for your sit:

"God is not just love (1 John 4:16) but also absolute faithfulness and hope itself. And the energy of this faithfulness and hope flows out from the Creator toward all created beings producing all growth, healing, and every springtime.
No one religion will ever encompass the depth of such faith.
No ethnicity has a monopoly on such hope.
No nationality can control or limit this Flow of such universal love."
(page 22)

- Continue your sit in silence—focusing on your breath, connecting with your body, or by practicing any other method with which you are familiar.
- If a contemplative sit is new to you, one approach is to try not to let your attention attach to any thoughts, feelings, or sensations. Allow thoughts, feelings, and sensations to arise, exist, and then fall away while you keep your attention open and large, connecting to that larger field.
- Remember, there is no goal. There is no right or wrong way— simply *be* present to what *is* in the moment.

Once finished, you may wish to journal your reflections on this experience.

TWO

Accepting That You Are Fully Accepted

1. *Lectio* Practice

Introductory quote:

> "Have you ever noticed that the expression 'the light of the world' is
> used to describe the Christ (John 8:12), but that Jesus also applies
> the same phrase to us? (Matthew 5:14, 'You are the light of the
> world.') Few preachers ever pointed that out to me." (page 31)

The text for this *Lectio* Practice is:

"You are the light of the world."

1. With the first reading, allow yourself to *settle in* to the exercise and
    familiarize yourself with the words. Read the text out loud, very
    slowly and clearly. Pause for a breath or two before moving on.

2. For the second reading, *listen* from a centered heart space and
    notice any word or phrase that stands out to you.

3. After a few moments of silence, read the text a third time, *reflecting* on how this word or phrase is connected to your current life experience. Take a minute to linger over this word or phrase, "to focus on it until it engages your body, your heart, your awareness of the physical [and unseen] world around you." (page 8)

    You may want to speak a response aloud or write something in your journal.

4. For the final reading, *respond* with a prayer or expression of what you have experienced, inviting the infinite wisdom of God to support you in places of unknowing, confusion, desire, or hope.

2. Reflection

Read this quotation, noticing what resonates with you and what you resist:

> "In the Gospels of Matthew, Mark, and Luke, Jesus almost always calls himself 'the Son of the Human,' or just 'Everyman,' using this expression a total of eighty-seven times. But in John's Gospel, dated somewhere between A.D. 90 and 110, the voice of Christ steps forward to do almost all of the speaking . . . 'I am the way, the truth, and the life' (John 14:6) or 'Before Abraham ever was, I am' (John 8:58). . . . If these are the words of the Eternal Christ, then 'I am the way, the truth, and the life' is a very fair statement that should neither offend nor threaten anyone. After all, Jesus is *not* talking about joining or excluding any group; rather, he is describing *the 'Way' by which all humans and all religions must allow matter and Spirit to operate as one.*" (page 26)

3. Embodiment

> "The full Christian story is saying that Jesus died, and Christ 'arose'—yes, still as Jesus, but now also as *the Corporate Personality who includes and reveals all of creation in its full purpose and goal.* . . . Most Catholics and Protestants still think of the incarnation as a one-time and one-person event having to do only with the person of Jesus of Nazareth, instead of a cosmic event that has soaked all of history in the Divine Presence from the very beginning." (pages 27–28)

Take a few minutes to open yourself to the Divine Presence being soaked in the place where you are reading this.

> ▸ Pay attention to what you can see around you and to what you can hear.

> "The Eastern church has a sacred word for this process, which we in the West call *'incarnation' or 'salvation.'* They call it *'divinization' (theosis).* If that sounds provocative, know that they are only building on 2 Peter 1:4, where the author says, 'He has given us something very great and wonderful . . . you are *able to share the divine nature!'* This is Christianity's core good news and only transformative message." (pages 27–28)

> ▸ Reflect for a moment on this notion that you are, right now, *"able to share the divine nature."* How do you respond? What thoughts, emotions, or sensations are arising?

4. Reflection

Take a minute to write down anything that resonates with you from these quotations:

"The only people that Jesus seemed to exclude were precisely those who refused to know they were ordinary sinners like everyone else. *The only thing he excluded was exclusion itself.* . . . Think about what all of this means for everything we sense and know about God." (page 34)

"We must be honest and humble about this: Many people of other faiths, like Sufi masters, Jewish prophets, many philosophers, and Hindu mystics, have lived in light of the Divine encounter better than many Christians. And why would a God worthy of the name God not care about *all* of the children?" (page 34)

"I fully believe, however, that *there has never been a single soul who was not possessed by the Christ, even in the ages when Jesus was not.* Why would you want your religion, or your God, to be any smaller than that?" (page 36)

"Our complete and happy inclusion of the Jewish scriptures inside of the Christian canon ought to have served as a structural and definitive statement about Christianity's movement toward radical inclusivity. How did we miss that? No other religion does that." (page 35)

▸ Now take a minute to write down anything that is difficult to understand or to accept from these same quotations.

▸ Which teachings and life experiences have most shaped your reactions?

5. Reflection

"The leap of faith that orthodox Christians made from the earliest period was the belief that this eternal Christ presence truly was speaking through the person of Jesus . . . for if the union of God and humankind is 'true' in Jesus, there is hope that it might be true in all of us too." (page 27)

"As long as we keep God imprisoned in a retributive frame instead of a restorative frame, we really have no substantial good news; it is neither good nor new, but the same old tired story line of history. We pull God down to our level." (pages 28–29)

"Faith at its essential core is *accepting that you are accepted!* We cannot deeply know ourselves without also knowing the One who made us, and we cannot fully accept ourselves without accepting God's radical acceptance of every part of us." (page 29)

- ▸ What parts of yourself has religion encouraged you to reject? Do you struggle to accept yourself as you are today?

- ▸ Take a few minutes to reflect on the impact this has had on your life.

Read the following line aloud, as many times as it takes, until something stirs within you:

"I cannot fully accept myself without accepting God's radical acceptance of every part of me."

- ▸ If it feels appropriate, you may want to pray (with words or in silence) on this theme of self-acceptance.

6. *Lectio* Practice

Introductory quotes:

"'The true light that enlightens every person *was coming (erxomenon)* into the world' (John 1:9). In other words, we're talking not about a one-time Big Bang in nature or a one-time incarnation in Jesus, but an ongoing, progressive movement continuing in the ever-unfolding creation. Incarnation did not just happen two thousand years ago. It has been working throughout the entire arc of time, and will continue. This is expressed in the common phrase the 'Second Coming of Christ,' which was unfortunately read as a threat ('Wait till your Dad gets home!'), whereas it should more accurately be spoken of as the 'Forever Coming of Christ,' which is anything but a threat. In fact, *it is the ongoing promise of eternal resurrection.*" (page 32)

"Christ is the light that allows people to see things in their fullness. The precise and intended effect of such a light is to see Christ everywhere else. In fact, that is my only definition of a true Christian. *A mature Christian sees Christ in everything and everyone else.*" (page 33)

The text for this *Lectio* Practice is:

"A mature Christian sees Christ in everything and everyone else."

1. With the first reading, allow yourself to *settle in* to the exercise and familiarize yourself with the words. Read the text out loud, very slowly and clearly. Pause for a breath or two before moving on.

2. For the second reading, *listen* from a centered heart space and notice any word or phrase that stands out to you.

3. After a few moments of silence, read the text a third time, *reflecting* on how this word or phrase is connected to your current life experience. Take a minute to linger over this word or phrase, "to focus on it until it engages your body, your heart, your awareness of the physical [and unseen] world around you." (page 8)

You may want to speak a response aloud or write something in your journal.

4.   For the final reading, *respond* with a prayer or expression of what you have experienced, inviting the infinite wisdom of God to support you in places of unknowing, confusion, desire, or hope.

7. Contemplative Sit

Leading in with the quotation below, practice a contemplative sit. You may wish to set a timer or digital prayer bell for 5, 10, or 20 minutes, so that you know when to finish.

Seat yourself in a quiet area. Once you are settled, read the passage aloud—this is the opening text for your sit:

> "To be loved by Jesus enlarges our heart capacity. To be loved by the Christ enlarges our *mental* capacity. We need both a Jesus and a Christ, in my opinion, to get the full picture. A truly transformative God—for both the individual and history—needs to be experienced as both personal and universal." (page 36)

> *"You are a child of God, and always will be, even when you don't believe it."* (page 37)

- ▸ Notice any tightness in your shoulders and neck and allow any tension in your muscles to relax.
- ▸ Allow your back to rest in an aligned, neutral position.
- ▸ Ground yourself and allow your breathing to settle. Then read the following aloud, pausing between each sentence:

> "I am not trying to 'achieve' anything. There are no goals. I am simply becoming aware of this moment. Becoming aware of my presence

in this moment. As I notice any distractions, thoughts, judgments, decisions, ideas that cross my mind, I let them go for now, focusing instead on my moment-by-moment experience of being present to What Is. God's Presence. the Larger Field. *En Cristo.*

"As I become distracted, frustrated, or confused, I consciously return to offering my moment-by-moment presence to God's Presence. God's Presence is already within me, whether I'm aware of it or not. No offering up is needed—I am offering in. Into the silence. Into each moment that I sit in contemplation.

"*'You are a child of God, and always will be, even when you don't believe it.'*" [Pause]

▸ Ring a prayer bell to indicate that the contemplative sit has begun.

Silence for 5, 10, or 20 minutes

Once the closing prayer bell or timer sounds, briefly write down what this experience was like for you.

8. Reflection

"Remember what God said to Moses: 'I AM Who I AM' (Exodus 3:14). *God is clearly not tied to a name,* nor does [God] seem to want us to tie the Divinity to any one name. . . . The Christ is always way too much for us, larger than any one era, culture, empire, or religion. . . . Jesus by himself has usually been limited by the evolution of human consciousness in these first two thousand years, and held captive by culture, by nationalism, and by Christianity's own cultural captivity to a white, bourgeois, and Eurocentric worldview. Up to now, we have not been carrying history too well, because 'there stood among us one we did not recognize,' 'one who came after me, because he existed before me' (John 1:26, 30). He came in mid-tone skin, from the underclass, a male body with a female soul, from an often hated religion, and living on the very cusp between East and West. No one owns him, and no one ever will." (page 35)

- ▸ What cultural and religious baggage has prevented you from more fully recognizing Christ in your day-to-day life?
- ▸ If you were to drop an item of such baggage, how would this impact your daily life and personal relationships?
- ▸ How would this affect the way you engage in life?

9. Reflection

"The point of the Christian life is not to distinguish oneself from the ungodly, but to stand in radical solidarity with everyone and everything else. This is the full, final, and intended effect of the incarnation—symbolized by its finality in the cross, which is *God's great act of solidarity instead of judgment*. Without a doubt, Jesus perfectly exemplified this seeing, and thus passed it on to the rest of history. This is how we are to imitate Christ, the good Jewish man who saw and called forth the divine in Gentiles like the Syro-Phoenician woman and the Roman centurions who followed him; in Jewish tax collectors who collaborated with the Empire; in zealots who opposed it; in sinners of all stripes; in eunuchs, pagan astrologers, and all those 'outside the law.' Jesus had no trouble whatsoever with *otherness*. In fact, these 'lost sheep' found out they were not lost to him at all, and tended to become his best followers. . . . In my opinion, his aliveness made it so much easier for people to trust their own aliveness and thus relate to God, because *like knows like*. Some call it *morphic resonance*." (page 33)

- Can you notice people/groups in your life or your community against whom you stand in judgment? When you reflect on Jesus, can you find a sense of his solidarity with them?

- In what ways *would you like* to join Jesus and stand with them in solidarity?

- What *will* you do to stand with them in solidarity?

10. Imagination Exercise

You may find it helpful to revisit "Staying within Your Comfort Zone" (page 23) prior to undertaking this exercise.

> "We need to look at Jesus until we can look out at the world with his kind of eyes. The world no longer trusts Christians who 'love Jesus' but do not seem to love anything else. *In Jesus Christ, God's own broad, deep, and all-inclusive worldview is made available to us.*" (page 32)

- Think of a person with whom you would like to express God's all-inclusive love. (Pause until you have thought of just one person.)

- Imagine that this person is here with you now, either standing or sitting across from you. (If you picture them sitting, you might want to place a chair for them and imagine them sitting with you.)

- Take a few moments of silence with this person. Notice what they are wearing and how they are sitting. What impression do you have of them? Speak out your answers so you can hear your thoughts aloud.

- Paying particular attention to this person's facial expression and body language, ask them, "How has life been for you so far?" "What is it like 'to walk in your shoes'?"

- What do you imagine is their response? Are they willing to share with you? Repeat back to them what you see and hear in your imagination (it might be helpful to use phrases that begin with, "I see that you are . . . ," "I hear that you feel . . . ," etc.). Take your time and say as much or as little as you wish.

When you have finished speaking, pause for a few moments.

- Now take a minute to notice what is going on within yourself:

  - What sensations are you experiencing in your body?
  - What emotions are you feeling?
  - What are you thinking? What's now dawning on you?
  - Where might you sense God's all-inclusive divine love and solidarity within this experience?

- Reflect on how you would like to express solidarity with this person. If you feel ready, go back into your scene and offer that expression.

Once you have finished speaking, pause for a final few moments.

- When you feel like the Imagination Exercise is drawing to a natural conclusion, thank the person for being present with you and say goodbye to them, perhaps even opening and closing a door to signify their departure.

This could be a good time to do some journaling, get some fresh air, engage with nature, interact with animals, speak to a friend, or do anything else that is helpful for you to relax before moving on to Chapter 3.

THREE

Revealed in Us—*as* Us

"Paul rarely, if ever, quotes Jesus himself directly. Rather, he writes from a place of trustful communication with the Divine Presence who blinded him on the road. Paul's driving mission was '*to demonstrate that Jesus was the Christ*' (Acts 9:22b), which is why we are called 'Christians.'" (page 40)

1. Reflection

"In Paul's story we find the archetypal spiritual pattern, wherein people move *from what they thought they always knew to what they now fully recognize*. The pattern reveals itself earlier in the Torah when Jacob 'wakes from his sleep' on the rock at Bethel and says, in effect, 'I found it, but it was here all the time! This is the very gate of heaven' (Genesis 28:16)." (page 40)

▸ Describe in your journal a moment when you moved "from what [you] thought [you] always knew to what [you] now fully recognize."

2. Reflection

"'God revealed his Son *in* me' (Galatians 1:16)." (pages 41–42)

"But let's note Paul's primary criterion for authentic faith, which is quite extraordinary: '*Examine yourselves to make sure you are in the faith. Test yourselves. Do you acknowledge that Jesus Christ is really in you? If not, you have failed the test*' (2 Corinthians 13:5–6)." (page 42)

"Paul merely took incarnationalism to its universal and logical conclusions. We see that in his bold exclamation, 'There is only Christ. He is everything and he is in everything' (Colossians 3:11). If I were to write that today, people would call me a pantheist (the universe is God), whereas I am really a pan*en*theist (God lies within all things, but also transcends them), exactly like both Jesus and Paul." (page 43)

"*The proof that you are a Christian is that you can see Christ everywhere else.*" (page 51)

- ▸ Take a couple of minutes to reflect on this notion of "pan*en*theist (God lies within all things, but also transcends them)."
- ▸ What does this evoke within you? You may want to journal your response.
- ▸ In what ways do you "*see Christ everywhere*"?

3. Contemplative Sit

Leading in with the quotation below, practice a contemplative sit. You may wish to set a timer or digital prayer bell for 5, 10, or 20 minutes, so that you know when to finish.

Seat yourself in a quiet area. Once you are settled, read the passage aloud—this is the opening text for your sit:

> "*I have never been separate from God, nor can I be, except in my mind.* I would love for you to bring this realization to loving consciousness! In fact, why not stop reading now, and just breathe and let it sink in. It is crucial that you know this experientially and at a cellular level—which is, in fact, a real way of knowing just as much as rational knowing. Its primary characteristic is that it is a non-dual and thus an open-ended way of knowing, which does not close down so quickly and so definitively as dualistic thought does." (pages 44–45)

▸ Notice any tightness in your shoulders and neck and allow any tension in your muscles to relax.

▸ Allow your back to rest in an aligned, neutral position.

▸ Ground yourself and allow your breathing to settle. Then read the following aloud, pausing between each sentence:

> "I am not trying to 'achieve' anything. There are no goals. I am simply becoming aware of this moment. Becoming aware of my presence in this moment. As I notice any distractions, thoughts, judgments, decisions, ideas that cross my mind, I let them go for now, focusing instead on my moment-by-moment experience of being present to What Is. God's Presence. The Larger Field. *En Cristo.*

> "As I become distracted, frustrated, or confused, I consciously return to offering my moment-by-moment presence to God's Presence. God's Presence is already within me, whether I'm aware of it or not. No offering up is needed—I am offering in. Into the silence. Into each moment that I sit in contemplation.

> "*I have never been separate from God, nor can I be, except in my mind.*"
> [Pause]

▸ Ring a prayer bell to indicate that the contemplative sit has begun.

Silence for 5, 10, or 20 minutes

Once the closing prayer bell or timer sounds, briefly write down what this experience was like for you.

4. Reflection

> "The term 'paradigm shift' describes a major switch in one's assumptions or viewpoint. . . . A religious paradigm shift was exactly what Jesus and Paul were initiating in their day. . . . The Universal Christ was just too big an idea, too monumental a shift for most of the first two thousand years. Humans prefer to see things in anecdotal and historical parts, even when such a view leads to incoherence, alienation, or hopelessness." (pages 46–47)

> "No doubt you're aware that many traditional Christians today consider the concept of universal anything—including salvation—heresy. Many do not even like the United Nations. And many Catholics and Orthodox Christians use the lines of ethnicity to determine who's in and who's out. I find these convictions quite strange for a religion that believes that 'one God created all things.'" (page 49)

> "This [1 Corinthians 15:28; Colossians 3:11; Colossians 1:19–20] is not heresy, universalism, or a cheap version of Unitarianism. This is the Cosmic Christ, who always was, who became incarnate in time, and who is still being revealed. *We would have helped history and individuals so much more if we had spent our time revealing how Christ is everywhere instead of proving that Jesus was God.*" (page 49)

▸ After reading these quotations, write down the first thoughts that come to mind. (Feel free to read over the quotations again before you begin to write.)

- To what extent do you agree or disagree that *"We would have helped history and individuals so much more if we had spent our time revealing how Christ is everywhere instead of proving that Jesus was God"*?

- What experiences from your own life have influenced your point of view?

5. Reflection

Take a few minutes to slowly meditate on this quotation:

> "You might wonder how, exactly, primitive peoples and pre-Christian civilizations could've had access to God. I believe it was through the universal and normal transformative journeys of *great love and great suffering*, which all individuals have undergone from the beginnings of the human race. Only great love and great suffering are strong enough to take away our imperial ego's protections and open us to authentic experiences of transcendence. The Christ, especially when twinned with Jesus, is a clear message about *universal love and necessary suffering as the divine pattern—* starting with the three persons of the Trinity, where *God is said to be both endlessly outpouring and self-emptying*." (page 50)

- How has your experience of great love and great suffering shaped your own life, both in the choices you have made and in the things you have experienced?

"It's important to remember that Paul, like us, never knew Jesus in the flesh. Like him, we only know the Christ through observing and honoring the depth of our own human experience. *When you can honor and receive your own moment of sadness or fullness as a gracious participation in the eternal sadness or fullness of God, you are beginning to recognize yourself as a participating member of this one universal Body. You are moving from I to We."* (page 42)

▸ Drawing on your answers to the question above, take a minute to prayerfully *"honor and receive your own moment of sadness or fullness as a gracious participation in the eternal sadness or fullness of God."*

6. Presence Exercise

"Anything that draws you out of yourself in a positive way—for all practical purposes—is operating as God for you at that moment. **How else can the journey begin? How else are you drawn forward . . . ? God needs something to seduce you out and beyond yourself, so God uses three things in particular: goodness, truth, and beauty."** (page 52)

"When you look your dog in the face, for example, as I often looked at my black Labrador, Venus, I truly believe you are seeing another incarnation of the Divine Presence, the Christ. When you look at any other person, a flower, a honeybee, a mountain—anything—you are seeing the incarnation of God's love for you and the universe you call home." (page 52)

▸ What experiences of goodness, truth, and beauty have drawn you out of yourself in a positive way? Can you connect to God in that experience? What does that feel like?

Create a plan to go and engage in an activity that has the possibility of leading you to one of those experiences. Whether it's nature-based, service-based, relational, or an intellectual, athletic, creative, or aesthetic pursuit, put the book down and

"Pause to focus on [and experience] an incarnation of God's love apparent . . . right now. You must risk it!" (page 52)

"It is so important to taste, touch, and trust such moments." (page 53)

After you have gone through the Presence Exercise, answer the following questions:

- Did you freely engage in this exercise from the outset or did you resist it?
- Did you experience the goodness, truth, or beauty you expected or did something unexpected happen?
- What did you notice about yourself from this experience? What did you notice about the world?

You may wish to write down any insights in your journal.

7. Engaging with the Environment

"Without a Shared and Big Story, we all retreat into private individualism for a bit of sanity and safety. Perhaps the primary example of our lack of attention to the Christ Mystery can be seen in the way we continue to pollute and ravage planet earth, the very thing we all stand on and live from. Science now appears to love and respect physicality more than most religion does! No wonder that *science and business have taken over as the major explainers of meaning* for the vast majority of people today (even many who still go to church). We Christians did not take this world seriously, I am afraid, because our notion of God or salvation didn't include or honor the physical universe. And now, I am afraid, the world does not take us seriously." (page 46)

- How have you been disconnected from a vision of God or salvation that honors the physical universe?

- How might you reclaim this vision in your own life?

Take three minutes to brainstorm any practical steps you could take to affect a positive sense of Shared and Big Story. For example, notice how much trash you produce and consider ways you might generate less, use energy-efficient lightbulbs, organize a street/beach/forest cleanup with friends and neighbors, volunteer at an animal shelter, grow your own herbs and vegetables, recycle, start using a composting bin, lobby your local politicians regarding a pressing environmental issue, etc.

- What one step will you take?

- When will you take this step?

- How will this move you from private individualism toward a Shared and Big Story?

8. *Lectio* Practice

Prepare for the *Lectio* by reading these quotations and pondering the question:

> "*En Cristo* seems to be Paul's code word for *the gracious, participatory experience of salvation*, the path that he so urgently wanted to share with the world. Succinctly put, this identity means *humanity has never been separate from God*—unless and except by its own negative choice. All of us, without exception, are living inside of a cosmic identity, already in place, that is driving and guiding us forward. We are all *en Cristo*, willingly or unwillingly, happily or unhappily, consciously or unconsciously." (page 43)

"Our circles of belonging tend to either expand or constrict as life goes on. . . . Our patterns of relating, once set, determine the trajectories for our whole lives. If we are inherently skeptical and suspicious, the focus narrows. If we are hopeful and trusting, the focus continues to expand." (page 51)

- Do you tend to be more hopeful and trusting or more skeptical and suspicious within your circles of belonging?

Introductory quote for *Lectio*:

"In God you do not include less and less; you always see and love more and more. The more you transcend your small ego, the more you can include. 'Unless the single grain of wheat dies, it remains just a single grain. But if it does, it will bear much fruit,' Jesus Christ says (John 12:24)." (page 52)

The text for this *Lectio* Practice is:

"Unless the single grain of wheat dies, it remains just a single grain. But if it does, it will bear much fruit."

1. With the first reading, allow yourself to *settle in* to the exercise and familiarize yourself with the words. Read the text out loud, very slowly and clearly. Pause for a breath or two before moving on.

2. For the second reading, *listen* from a centered heart space and notice any word or phrase that stands out to you.

3. After a few moments of silence, read the text a third time, *reflecting* on how this word or phrase is connected to your current life experience. Take a minute to linger over this word or phrase, "to focus on it until it engages your body, your heart,

your awareness of the physical [and unseen] world around you."
(page 8)

You may want to speak a response aloud or write something in
your journal.

4.   For the final reading, *respond* with a prayer or expression of what
you have experienced, inviting the infinite wisdom of God to
support you in places of unknowing, confusion, desire, or hope.

FOUR

Original Goodness

1. Reflection

"But in the mid-nineteenth century, grasping for the certitude and authority the church was quickly losing in the face of rationalism and scientism, Catholics declared the Pope to be 'infallible,' and Evangelicals decided the Bible was 'inerrant,' despite the fact that we had gotten along for most of eighteen hundred years without either belief. In fact, these claims would have seemed idolatrous to most early Christians." (page 58)

- Notice what you resist and what you are drawn toward as you read about infallibility and inerrancy.
- What memories or images do these terms evoke?

"Creation—be it planets, plants, or pandas—was not just a warm-up act for the human story or the Bible. The natural world is its own good and sufficient story, if we can only learn to see it with humility and love. That takes contemplative practice, stopping our busy and superficial minds long enough to see the beauty,

allow the truth, and protect the inherent goodness of what it is."
(page 58)

- What recent experiences do you have of seeing the natural world "with humility and love"?

- What effect did this have on you?

2. Reflection

"The cottonwood [tree] is easily the finest work of art that we have at the [CAC], and its asymmetrical beauty makes it a perfect specimen for one of our organization's core messages: *Divine perfection is precisely the ability to include what seems like imperfection.* Before we come inside to pray, work, or teach any theology, [the] giant presence [of the cottonwood tree] has already spoken a silent sermon over us." (pages 55–56)

Take a couple of minutes to reflect on the imperfections and the circuitous branches of your own life.

- What experiences of "imperfection" have unexpectedly shaped your life in significant ways?

- What would it mean to you to be able to accept and include all of these experiences as "Divine perfection"?

3. Memories

"Perhaps for you, it occurred at a lake or by the seashore, hiking in the mountains, in a garden listening to a mourning dove, even at a busy street corner. I am convinced that when received, such innate theology grows us, expands us, and enlightens us almost effortlessly. All other God talk seems artificial and heady in comparison." (page 56)

- Have you ever had an encounter like this in nature?

- Describe one of those experiences in your journal. What stands out from your memory? Can you feel God present in that experience?

4. Reflection

"The concept of *original sin* entered the Christian mind . . . first put forth by Augustine in the fifth century, but never mentioned in the Bible—we emphasized that human beings were born into 'sin' because Adam and Eve 'offended God' by eating from the 'tree of the knowledge of good and evil.' . . . This strange concept of original sin does not match the way we usually think of sin, which is normally a matter of personal responsibility and culpability." (page 61)

"Most of the world's great religions start with some sense of primal goodness in their creation stories. The Judeo-Christian tradition beautifully succeeded at this, with the Genesis record telling us that God called creation 'good' five times in Genesis 1:10–22, and even 'very good.'" (page 61)

"But after Augustine, most Christian theologies shifted from the positive vision of Genesis 1 to the darker vision of Genesis 3—the so-called fall, or what I am calling the 'problem.' Instead of embracing God's master plan for humanity and creation—what we Franciscans still call the 'Primacy of Christ'—Christians shrunk our image of both Jesus and Christ, and our 'Savior' became a mere Johnny-come-lately 'answer' to the problem of sin, a problem that we had largely created ourselves. That's a very limited role for Jesus. His *death* instead of his *life* was defined as saving us!" (pages 61–62)

▸ Before reading this chapter, what had you been taught and what did you believe regarding this "problem of sin"?

▸ As you intuitively reflect on these quotations and your own experience of faith and spirituality, what understanding of sin is making sense to you right now?

5. Contemplative Sit

Leading in with the quotation below, practice a contemplative sit. You may wish to set a timer or digital prayer bell for 5, 10, or 20 minutes, so that you know when to finish.

Seat yourself in a quiet area. Once you are settled, read the passage aloud—this is the opening text for your sit:

"God is not bound by the human presumption that we are the center of everything, and creation did not actually demand or need Jesus (or *us*, for that matter) to confer additional sacredness upon it. From the first moment of the Big Bang, nature was revealing the glory and goodness of the Divine Presence; it must be seen as a gratuitous gift and not a necessity. Jesus came to live in its midst, and enjoy life in all its natural variations, and thus be our model and exemplar. *Jesus is the gift that honored the gift*, you might say." (page 56)

▸ Notice any tightness in your shoulders and neck and allow any tension in your muscles to relax.

▸ Allow your back to rest in an aligned, neutral position.

▸ Ground yourself and allow your breathing to settle. Then read the following aloud, pausing between each sentence:

"I am not trying to 'achieve' anything. There are no goals. I am simply becoming aware of this moment. Becoming aware of my presence in this moment. As I notice any distractions, thoughts, judgments, decisions, ideas that cross my mind, I let them go for now, focusing instead on my moment-by-moment experience of being present to What Is. God's Presence. The Larger Field. *En Cristo*.

"As I become distracted, frustrated, or confused, I consciously return to offering my moment-by-moment presence to God's Presence. God's Presence is already within me, whether I'm aware of it or not. No offering up is needed—I am offering in. Into the silence. Into each moment that I sit in contemplation.

"*I have never been separate from God, nor can I be, except in my mind.*" [Pause]

▸ Ring a prayer bell to indicate that the contemplative sit has begun.

Silence for 5, 10, or 20 minutes

Once the closing prayer bell or timer sounds, briefly write down what this experience was like for you.

6. Reflection

> "In one way, the doctrine of 'original sin' *was* good and helpful in that it taught us *not to be surprised at the frailty and woundedness that we all carry.* Just as goodness is inherent and shared, so it seems with evil. And this is, in fact, a very merciful teaching. Knowledge of our shared wound ought to free us from the burden of unnecessary—and individual—guilt or shame, and help us to be forgiving and compassionate with ourselves and with one another." (page 62)

Thinking of an area of your life where you feel frail or wounded, reflect on this notion that you share this "frailty and woundedness" with everybody else. (Others may not understand your experiences of this and you may not understand theirs, but you share a common "burden.")

Feelings
- What emotions does this stir within you?
- What sensations do you notice in your body? Write down whatever comes to you.

Connection
- In what ways do you feel connected with others?
- How does this affect any feelings of "unnecessary—and individual—guilt or shame"?

Compassion
- In what ways are you forgiving and compassionate toward yourself?
- In what ways are you forgiving and compassionate toward others?

Take a few minutes and write down your answers.

▸ What does this exercise evoke in you?

7. *Lectio* **Practice**

> "St. Bonaventure (1221–1274) taught that *to work up to loving God, start by loving the very humblest and simplest things, and then move up from there.*" (page 57)

> "I encourage you to apply this spiritual insight quite literally. Don't start by trying to love God, or even people; love rocks and elements first, move to trees, then animals, and then humans. . . . It might be the only way to love, because *how you do anything is how you do everything.*" (page 57)

> "The message [of the Great Chain of Being] was that if you failed to recognize the Presence in any one link of the chain, the whole sacred universe would fall apart." (pages 57–58)

The text for this *Lectio* Practice is:

"How you do anything is how you do everything."

1. With the first reading, allow yourself to *settle in* to the exercise and familiarize yourself with the words. Read the text out loud, very slowly and clearly. Pause for a breath or two before moving on.

2. For the second reading, *listen* from a centered heart space and notice any word or phrase that stands out to you.

3. After a few moments of silence, read the text a third time, *reflecting* on how this word or phrase is connected to your current life experience. Take a minute to linger over this word or phrase, "to focus on it until it engages your body, your heart,

your awareness of the physical [and unseen] world around you."
(page 8)

You may want to speak a response aloud or write something in
your journal.

4. For the final reading, *respond* with a prayer or expression of what
    you have experienced, inviting the infinite wisdom of God to
    support you in places of unknowing, confusion, desire, or hope.

    Allow the text to sink in and settle within your whole being
    before moving on.

Either now or at some point in the next day or so, take a walk and
focus on something natural in your world. Find the "link of the chain"
that's right in front of you now and allow yourself to love it.

8. Reflection

"But after Augustine, most Christian theologies shifted from the
positive vision of Genesis 1 to the darker vision of Genesis 3—the
so-called fall, or what I am calling the 'problem.'" (page 61)

"The whole dynamic, in fact, is called the Velcro/Teflon theory of
the mind. We are more attracted to the problem than to the solution, you might say." (page 64)

▸ Where have you noticed this dynamic at play in your life?

"The only way, then, to increase authentic spirituality is to
deliberately practice actually enjoying a positive response and
a grateful heart. And the benefits are very real. By following
through on conscious choices, we can rewire our responses toward

love, trust, and patience. Neuroscience calls this '*neuroplasticity*.'"
(page 64)

"A wonderful description of this act of the will is found in Philippians 4:4–9, where Paul writes, 'Rejoice in the Lord *always* [italics
added].'" (page 64)

"*I have never met a truly compassionate or loving human being who did
not have a foundational and even deep trust in the inherent goodness
of human nature.*" (page 63)

▸ Name five things you are grateful for right now. They can be
  simple things, such as being able to breathe, having access to
  clean water, or having someone in your life that you love.

▸ For each of the five, spend fifteen seconds being grateful—
  thinking, thanking, and appreciating.

9. Reflection

"We do have to choose to trust reality and even our physicality,
which is to finally trust ourselves. Our readiness to *not* trust ourselves is surely one of our recurring sins. Yet so many sermons tell
us to *never* trust ourselves, to *only* trust God. That is far too dualistic. How can a person who does not trust himself know how to
trust at all? Trust, like love, is of one piece. (By the way, at this point
in history, '*trust*' is probably a much more helpful and descriptive
word than 'faith,' a notion that has become far too misused, intel-
lectualized, and even banal.)" (page 66)

▸ Reflect on something that is happening in your life where *you* are
  struggling to have faith, finding it difficult to trust. It might be
  a relational challenge, a lack of confidence in your role at work,
  not being certain of a choice you have to make, etc. Be sure to

choose a situation where the onus is on you and not on anybody else.

▸ Read over the above quotation and notice what thoughts and ideas come to mind regarding this situation.

▸ Now take a minute to pray for this situation by consciously handing it over to God and then repeating the following three lines out loud several times (repeat them until you feel ready to move on):

Help me to "trust in inner coherence itself. 'It all means something!' (Faith)"

Help me to "trust that this coherence is positive and going somewhere good (Hope)"

Help me to "trust that this coherence includes me and even defines me (Love)" (page 66)

10. Reflection

"For the planet and for all living beings to move forward, we can rely on nothing less than *an inherent original goodness and a universally shared dignity*. Only then can we build, because the foundation is strong, and is itself good. Surely this is what Jesus meant when he told us to 'dig and dig deep, and build your house on rock' (Luke 6:48)." (page 67)

"Our postmodern world seems highly subject to cynicism, skepticism, and what it does *not* believe in. . . . We 'believers' must take at least partial responsibility for aiming our culture in this sad direction. *The best criticism of the bad is still the practice of the better.*" (page 67)

"We must reclaim Jesus as an inclusive Savior instead of an exclu-sionary Judge, as a Christ who holds history together as the cosmic Alpha and Omega. Then, both history and the individual can live inside of a collective safety and an assured success. Some would call this the very shape of salvation." (page 68)

- Taking this notion that *"the best criticism of the bad is still the practice of the better,"* notice where your mind goes into criticizing individuals or systems in the coming days. What would you like to stop thinking, doing, and saying?

Spend some time in reflection and journaling your responses to these questions:

- In what ways do you "rely on nothing less than *an inherent original goodness and a universally shared dignity*"?
- What action would be the *"practice of the better"* that will most benefit you and others?

FIVE

Love Is the Meaning

1. *Lectio* Practice

The text for this *Lectio* Practice is:

> "'If we knew how to *adore*, then nothing could truly disturb our peace. We would travel through the world with the tranquility of the *great rivers*. But only if we know how to *adore*.'" (Eloi Leclerc, pages 74–75)

1. With the first reading, allow yourself to *settle in* to the exercise and familiarize yourself with the words. Read the text out loud, very slowly and clearly. Pause for a breath or two before moving on.

2. For the second reading, *listen* from a centered heart space and notice any word or phrase that stands out to you.

3. After a few moments of silence, read the text a third time, *reflecting* on how this word or phrase is connected to your current life

experience. Take a minute to linger over this word or phrase, "to focus on it until it engages your body, your heart, your awareness of the physical [and unseen] world around you." (page 8)

You may want to speak a response aloud or write something in your journal.

4. For the final reading, *respond* with a prayer or expression of what you have experienced, inviting the infinite wisdom of God to support you in places of unknowing, confusion, desire, or hope.

Allow the text to sink in and settle within your whole being before moving on.

2. Reflection

Read the following quotations, noticing Fr. Richard's term, "positive flow." What do you sense?

"For Pierre Teilhard de Chardin . . . love is the very physical structure of the Universe. That is a very daring statement, especially for a scientist to make. . . . Gravity, atomic bonding, orbits, cycles, photosynthesis, ecosystems, force fields, electromagnetic fields, sexuality, human friendship, animal instinct, and evolution all reveal an energy that is attracting all things and beings to one another." (page 69)

"Love . . . is so simple that it is hard to teach in words, yet we all know it when we see it. After all, there is not a Native, Hindu, Buddhist, Jewish, Islamic, or Christian way of loving. . . . We all know positive flow when we see it, and we all know resistance and coldness when we feel it." (page 70)

"Have you ever deliberately befriended a person standing alone at a party? Perhaps someone who was in no way attractive to you, or with whom you shared no common interests? That would be a small but real example of divine love flowing. Don't dismiss it as insignificant." (page 70)

▸ Take a few minutes to journal your response.

3. Reflection

"Religion . . . [is] more about waking up than about cleaning up. Early-stage religion tends to focus on cleaning up, which is to say, determining who meets the requirements for moral behavior and religious belief. But Jesus . . . [refused] to enforce or even bother with what he considered secondary issues like the Sabbath, ritual laws, purity codes, membership requirements, debt codes, on and on. He saw they were only 'human commandments,' which far too often took the place of love. (See especially Matthew 15:3, 6–9.) . . . Cleaning up is a result of waking up, but most of us put the cart before the horse." (pages 72–73)

"When it comes to actual soul work, most attempts at policing and conforming are largely useless. It took me most of my life as a confessor, counselor, and spiritual director to be honest and truly helpful with people about this. Mere obedience is far too often a detour around actual love. Obedience is usually about cleaning up, love is about waking up." (page 73)

▸ How much of your faith experience has been focused on "cleaning up"?

▸ What difference would it make—to you and to others—if you were to focus a little more on "waking up"?

4. Reflection

"'God does not offer Himself to our finite beings as a thing all complete and ready to be embraced. For us, He is eternal discovery and eternal growth. The more we think we understand Him, the more he reveals himself as otherwise. The more we think we hold him, the further He withdraws, drawing us into the depths of himself.'" (Pierre Teilhard de Chardin, page 78)

"*God creates the pullback too,* 'hiding his face' as it was called by so many mystics and Scriptures. God creates a vacuum that God alone can fill. Then God waits to see if we will trust our God partner to eventually fill the space in us, which now has grown even more spacious and receptive. This is the central theme of darkness, necessary doubt, or what the mystics called 'God withdrawing his love.'" (page 78)

▸ How does this fit your experience of God?

"I must be honest with you here about my own life. For the last ten years I have had little spiritual 'feeling,' neither consolation nor desolation. Most days, I've had to simply choose to believe, to love, and to trust. The simple kindness and gratitude of good people produces a momentary 'good feeling' in me, but even this goodness I do not know how to hold on to." (pages 78–79)

▸ What is your reaction to reading about Fr. Richard's experiences of God "hiding his face"?

5. Reflection

"*You might say that the Eternal Christ is the symbolic 'superconductor' of the Divine Energies into this world. Jesus ramps down the ohms so we*

can handle divine love and receive it through ordinary human mediums."
(page 76)

"To complete the circuit of Divine Love, we often need a moment
of awe, a person who evokes that electric conductivity, something
we can deeply respect, or even call 'Father' or 'Mother' or 'Lover' or
just 'beautiful.' Only then do we find the courage and confidence
to complete God's circuit from our side. This is why people know
they do not fully choose love; they fall into it, allow it, and then
receive its strong charge. The evidence that you are involved in
this flow will often seem two-sided." (pages 76–77)

Describe in your journal a time when you fell in love with something
or someone that you deeply respected.

- ▸ What was that experience like for you?
- ▸ Write a few paragraphs to/about that person/thing that express
  your experience of falling in love and being part of "the circuit of
  Divine Love."

6. Contemplative Sit

Leading in with the quotation below, practice a contemplative sit. You
may wish to set a timer or digital prayer bell for 5, 10, or 20 minutes,
so that you know when to finish.

Seat yourself in a quiet area. Once you are settled, read the passage
aloud—this is the opening text for your sit:

"You are simultaneously losing control and finding it." (page 77)

- ▸ Notice any tightness in your shoulders and neck and allow any
  tension in your muscles to relax.

- Allow your back to rest in an aligned, neutral position.
- Ground yourself and allow your breathing to settle. Then read the following aloud, pausing between each sentence:

"I am not trying to 'achieve' anything. There are no goals. I am simply becoming aware of this moment. Becoming aware of my presence in this moment. As I notice any distractions, thoughts, judgments, decisions, ideas that cross my mind, I let them go for now, focusing instead on my moment-by-moment experience of being present to What Is. God's Presence. The Larger Field. *En Cristo.*

"As I become distracted, frustrated, or confused, I consciously return to offering my moment-by-moment presence to God's Presence. God's Presence is already within me, whether I'm aware of it or not. No offering up is needed—I am offering in. Into the silence. Into each moment that I sit in contemplation.

"You are simultaneously losing control and finding it." [Pause]

- Ring a prayer bell to indicate that the contemplative sit has begun.

Silence for 5, 10, or 20 minutes

Once the closing prayer bell or timer sounds, briefly write down what this experience was like for you.

7. Reflection

"Humans seem to want, even need something (or someone) that we can give ourselves to totally, something that focuses and gathers our affections. We need at least one place where we can 'kneel and kiss the ground,' as Rumi, the Sufi poet and mystic, put it." (page 74)

"After years of counseling both religious and nonreligious people, it seems to me that most humans need a love object (which will then become a subject!) to keep themselves both sane and happy. That love object becomes our 'North Star,' serving as our moral compass and our reason to keep putting one foot in front of the other in a happy and hopeful way. All of us need someone or something to connect our hearts with our heads. Love grounds us by creating focus, direction, motivation, even joy—and if we don't find these things in love, we usually will try to find them in hate. Do you see the consequences of this unmet need in our population today?" (page 74)

Take a minute to answer Fr. Richard's question.

- What, in your own words, are "the consequences of this unmet need" in the place where you live?
- What could you do to help one other person find and embrace a "love object"?

8. Reflection

"Remember again, *God loves you by becoming you*, taking your side in the inner dialogue of self-accusation and defense. God loves you by turning your mistakes into grace, by constantly giving you back to yourself in a larger shape. God stands with you, and not against you, when you are tempted to shame or self-hatred. If your authority figures never did that for you, it can be hard to feel it or trust it. But you must experience this love at a cellular level at least once. (Remember, the only thing that separates you from God is *the thought* that you are separate from God!)" (pages 79–80)

"The receiving of love lets us know that there was indeed a Giver. And freedom to even ask for love is the beginning of the receiving. Thus Jesus

can rightly say, 'If you ask, you will receive' (Matthew 7:7–8). To ask is to open the conduit from your side. Your asking is only seconding the motion. The first motion is always from God." (page 80)

▸ What is it you want to ask of God? Take some time to pray, to journal, or to simply sit with this request of God.

SIX

A Sacred Wholeness

1. Contemplative Sit

> "At one point, Jung wrote, '*My pilgrim's progress has been to climb down a thousand ladders until I could finally reach out a hand of friendship to the little clod of earth that I am.*' Jung, a supposed unbeliever, knew that any authentic God experience takes a lot of humility and a lot of honesty. The proud cannot know God because God is not proud, but infinitely humble. Remember, only like can know like! A combination of humility and patient seeking is the best spiritual practice of all." (page 86)

- ▸ Take a few moments to sit with the quotation from Jung. What comes up for you?

Choose a phrase or full sentence from the quotation above and use it as the introductory text for a contemplative sit. You may wish to set a timer or digital prayer bell for 5, 10, or 20 minutes, so that you know when to finish.

- Seat yourself in a quiet area.

- Once you are settled, write out and read aloud the text you have selected as the introduction to your sit.

- Notice any tightness in your shoulders and neck and allow any tension in your muscles to relax.

- Allow your back to rest in an aligned, neutral position.

- Ground yourself and allow your breathing to settle. Then read the following aloud, pausing between each sentence:

"I am not trying to 'achieve' anything. There are no goals. I am simply becoming aware of this moment. Becoming aware of my presence in this moment. As I notice any distractions, thoughts, judgments, decisions, ideas that cross my mind, I let them go for now, focusing instead on my moment-by-moment experience of being present to What Is. God's Presence. The Larger Field. *En Cristo.*

"As I become distracted, frustrated, or confused, I consciously return to offering my moment-by-moment presence to God's Presence. God's Presence is already within me, whether I'm aware of it or not. No offering up is needed—I am offering in. Into the silence. Into each moment that I sit in contemplation."

- Ring a prayer bell to indicate that the contemplative sit has begun.

Silence for 5, 10, or 20 minutes

Once the closing prayer bell or timer sounds, briefly write down what this experience was like for you.

2. Reflection

"Without desiring to patronize her, I would identify Etty as a person Karl Rahner would've called an 'anonymous Christian,' someone who unravels the underlying mystery of incarnation better than most Christians I know. Such folks are much more common than Christians imagine, although they do not need that appellation. . . . She addressed God repeatedly in her diaries, regarding him not as an external savior, but as *a power she could nurture and feed inside of her.*" (pages 81–82)

"'Those two months behind barbed wire have been the two richest and most intense months of my life, in which my highest values were so deeply confirmed. I have learnt to love Westerbork.'" (Etty Hillesum, page 83)

"Etty Hillesum is but one example of another function of the Christ: a universally available 'voice' that calls all things to *become whole and true to themselves.* God's two main tools in this direction, from every appearance, seem to be great love and great suffering—and often great love that *invariably leads* to great suffering." (page 83)

▸ What do you make of Etty Hillesum's experience? What would you have been tempted to reject or not welcome if you were in her circumstances? How did things "*become whole and true to themselves*" for her?

▸ In your own experience, which has come first: great love leading to great suffering or great suffering leading to great love?

▸ How has this pattern affected your sense of becoming "whole and true"?

3. Reflection

"Many educated and sophisticated people are not willing to submit to indirect, subversive, and intuitive knowing, which is probably why they rely far too much on external law and ritual behavior to achieve their spiritual purposes." (pages 85–86)

"But think about it: If the incarnation is true, then *of course* God speaks to you through your own thoughts! As Joan of Arc brilliantly replied when the judge accused her of being the victim of her own imagination, 'How else would God speak to me?' Many of us have been trained to write off these inner voices as mere emotion, religious conditioning, or psychological manipulation. Perhaps they sometimes are, but often they are *not*." (page 86)

"And this is where embracing the Christ Mystery becomes utterly practical. *Without the mediation of Christ, we will be tempted to overplay the distance and the distinction between God and humanity.* But because of the incarnation, the supernatural is forever embedded in the natural, making the very distinction false. How good is that? This is why saints like Augustine, Teresa of Avila, and Carl Jung seem to fully equate the discovery of their own souls with the very discovery of God. It takes much of our life, much lived experience, to trust and allow such a process. But when it comes, *it will feel like a calm and humble ability to quietly trust yourself and trust God at the same time.* Isn't that what we all want?" (page 87)

Notice what resonates with you as you read about this "inner voice" of God.

- ▸ Pay particular attention to what you are drawn toward and what you resist in the quotations.

- ▸ Have you ever sensed this "inner voice" before? If so, what were the circumstances and how did you respond?

- What is your experience of having *"a calm and humble ability to quietly trust yourself and trust God at the same time"*?

4. Stream of Consciousness Exercise

Take between five and ten minutes for the following exercise. It is a good idea to set a timer so that you know when to finish.

- Sit in a comfortable position. Feel free to light a candle or choose a seat that has a view of the sky or of nature.

- Read over the following quotations a couple of times. Then allow your mind to wander wherever it will go.

- Don't edit this process; simply allow a "stream of consciousness" process to unfold, letting one thought flow into the next.

- You may want to record your thoughts in your journal, or as an audio recording.

"If any thought feels too harsh, shaming, or diminishing of yourself or others, it is not likely the voice of God. Trust me on that. That is simply *your* voice. Why do humans so often presume the exact opposite—that shaming voices are always from God, and grace voices are always the imagination? That is a self-defeating ('demonic'?) path. Yet, as a confessor and a spiritual director, I can confirm that this broken logic is the general norm. *If something comes toward you with grace and can pass through you and toward others with grace, you can trust it as the voice of God.*" (page 88)

"If a voice comes from accusation and leads to accusation, it is quite sim-ply the voice of the 'Accuser,' which is the literal meaning of the biblical word 'Satan.' Shaming, accusing, or blaming is simply not how God talks. It is how we talk. God is supremely nonviolent, and I have

learned that from the saints and mystics that I have read and met and heard about. That many holy people cannot be wrong." (page 89)

Once you have finished reading the passages a couple of times and have allowed your mind to wander wherever it will go, answer the following questions:

- What was the predominant tone of your thoughts—one of grace, trust, and compassion or one of shame, accusation, and blame?

- If you were to hear from God right now, to connect with the Larger Field and see things in their cosmic wholeness, what might you hear?

5. Reflection

"In his critique of his father and uncles, Jung recognized that many humans had become reflections of the punitive God they worshiped. A forgiving God allows us to recognize the good in the supposed bad, and the bad in the supposed perfect or ideal. *Any view of God as tyrannical or punitive tragically keeps us from admitting these seeming contradictions.*" (pages 84–85)

- In what ways are your interactions with others a reflection of the God you worship?

- Take a moment to pause and reflect on any ways your sense of the God you worship is being impacted by reading this book.

6. *Lectio* Practice

The text for this *Lectio* Practice is:

> "'*We must listen to what is supporting us. We must listen to what is encouraging us. We must listen to what is urging us. We must listen to what is alive in us.*'" (pages 88–89)

1. With the first reading, allow yourself to *settle in* to the exercise and familiarize yourself with the words. Read the text out loud, very slowly and clearly. Pause for a breath or two before moving on.

2. For the second reading, *listen* from a centered heart space and notice any word or phrase that stands out to you.

3. After a few moments of silence, read the text a third time, *reflecting* on how this word or phrase is connected to your current life experience. Take a minute to linger over this word or phrase, "to focus on it until it engages your body, your heart, your awareness of the physical [and unseen] world around you." (page 8)

    You may want to speak a response aloud or write something in your journal.

4. For the final reading, *respond* with a prayer or expression of what you have experienced, inviting the infinite wisdom of God to support you in places of unknowing, confusion, desire, or hope.

    Allow the text to sink in and settle within your whole being before moving on.

SEVEN

Going Somewhere Good

1. Reflection

Read the following quotation:

> "Anything called 'Good News' needs to reveal a universal pattern
> that can be relied upon, and not just clannish or tribal patterns
> that might be true on occasion. This is probably why Christian-
> ity's break with ethnic Judaism was inevitable, although never
> intended by either Jesus or Paul, and why by the early second
> century Christians were already calling themselves 'catholics' or
> 'the universals.'" (page 97)

- ► Where has Christianity maintained a sense of the universal
  and where has it reverted back to tribal patterns? Journal your
  response.

2. Contemplative Sit

Leading in with the quotation below, practice a contemplative sit. Now that you have some experience of a contemplative sit, you may wish to sit for a little longer. Set a timer or digital prayer bell for 10, 15, or 20 minutes, so that you know when to finish.

Seat yourself in a quiet area. Once you are settled, read the passage aloud—this is the opening text for your sit:

> "At the front of their consciousness was a belief that God is leading all of history somewhere larger and broader and better for all of humanity. Yet, after Jesus and Paul—except for occasional theologians like Gregory of Nyssa, Athanasius, Maximus the Confessor, and Francis of Assisi—the most widely accepted version of Christianity had little to do with the cosmos or creation, nature or even history. Our beliefs did not generally talk about the future, except in terms of judgment and apocalypse. This is no way to guide history forward; no way to give humanity hope, purpose, direction, or joy." (page 97)

- Notice any tightness in your shoulders and neck and allow any tension in your muscles to relax.
- Allow your back to rest in an aligned, neutral position.
- Ground yourself and allow your breathing to settle. Then read the following aloud, pausing between each sentence:

> "I am not trying to 'achieve' anything. There are no goals. I am simply becoming aware of this moment. Becoming aware of my presence in this moment. As I notice any distractions, thoughts, judgments, decisions, ideas that cross my mind, I let them go for now, focusing instead on my moment-by-moment experience of being present to What Is. God's Presence. The Larger Field. *En Cristo.*

"As I become distracted, frustrated, or confused, I consciously return to offering my moment-by-moment presence to God's Presence. God's Presence is already within me, whether I'm aware of it or not. No offering up is needed—I am offering in. Into the silence. Into each moment that I sit in contemplation.

"At the front of their consciousness was a belief that God is leading all of history somewhere larger and broader and better for all of humanity." [Pause]

▸ Ring a prayer bell to indicate that the contemplative sit has begun.

Silence for 10, 15, or 20 minutes

Once the closing prayer bell or timer sounds, briefly write down what this experience was like for you.

3. Reflection

"Jesus quite clearly believed in change. In fact, the first public word out of his mouth was the Greek imperative verb *metanoeite*, which literally translates as 'change your mind' or 'go beyond your mind' (Matthew 3:2, 4:17, and Mark 1:15). Unfortunately, in the fourth century, St. Jerome translated the word into Latin as *paenitentia* ('repent' or 'do penance'), initiating a host of moralistic connotations that have colored Christians' understanding of the Gospels ever since. The word *metanoeite*, however, is talking about *a primal change of mind, worldview, or your way of processing*—and only by corollary about a specific change in behavior. The common misunderstanding puts the cart before the horse; we think we can change a few externals while our underlying worldview often remains fully narcissistic and self-referential." (page 92)

- ▸ Take a few minutes to reflect on what you understood when you first heard the phrase "repent and believe the Good News."

- ▸ How is this similar to and different from the notion of changing your mind or your worldview?

4. Reflection

Take a couple of minutes to notice the first thoughts that come to mind as you read the following quotation:

> "All I know is that creationists and evolutionists do not have to be enemies. . . . True Christianity and true science are both trans-formational worldviews that place growth and development at their centers. Both endeavors, each in its own way, cooperate with some Divine Plan, and whether God is formally acknowledged may not be that important." (pages 99–100)

Sit with this C. G. Jung quotation for a few moments: *"Vocatus atque non vocatus, Deus aderit,* 'Invoked or not invoked, God is still present.'" (page 100)

- ▸ What does this evoke in you?

5. *Lectio* Practice

Introductory Text

> "Yet to believe that Jesus was raised from the dead is actually not a leap of faith. *Resurrection and renewal are, in fact, the universal and observable pattern of everything.* We might just as well use non-religious terms like 'springtime,' 'regeneration,' 'healing,' 'forgive-ness,' 'life cycles,' 'darkness,' and 'light.' If incarnation is real, then

resurrection in multitudinous forms is to be fully expected." (page 99)

The text for this *Lectio* Practice is:

"God *protects us into* and *through* death, just as the Father did with Jesus." (page 93)

1. With the first reading, allow yourself to *settle in* to the exercise and familiarize yourself with the words. Read the text out loud, very slowly and clearly. Pause for a breath or two before moving on.

2. For the second reading, *listen* from a centered heart space and notice any word or phrase that stands out to you.

3. After a few moments of silence, read the text a third time, *reflecting* on how this word or phrase is connected to your current life experience. Take a minute to linger over this word or phrase, "to focus on it until it engages your body, your heart, your awareness of the physical [and unseen] world around you." (page 8)

   You may want to speak a response aloud or write something in your journal.

4. For the final reading, *respond* with a prayer or expression of what you have experienced, inviting the infinite wisdom of God to support you in places of unknowing, confusion, desire, or hope.

   Allow the text to sink in and settle within your whole being before moving on.

6. Reflection

"When Jesus first announced 'change your mind,' he immediately challenged his apostles to leave both their jobs and their families (see Mark 1:20, Matthew 4:22). The change of mind had immediate and major social implications, leading young Jewish men to call two solidly conservative sacred cows—occupation and family—into full question. He did not tell them to attend the synagogue more often or to believe that he was God. Have you ever noted that Jesus never once speaks glowingly of the nuclear family, careers, or jobs? Check it out." (page 94)

"But growth language says it is appropriate to wait, trusting that *metanoeite*, or change of consciousness, can only come with time—and this patience ends up being the very shape of love." (page 96)

- Gently reflect on an area of your life where a "change of mind" would feel like both a relief and a challenge.

- If you were to trust yourself on this, what actions might flow from this instinct?

7. Engage

"*There is no such thing as a nonpolitical Christianity.* To refuse to critique the system or the status quo is to fully support it—which is a political act well disguised. Like Pilate, many Christians choose to wash their hands in front of the crowd and declare themselves innocent, saying with him, 'It is your concern' (Matthew 27:25). Pilate maintains his purity and Jesus pays the price." (page 94)

- In what ways are you critiquing "the system or the status quo" through your lifestyle and through your words?

"Going somewhere good means having to go through and with the bad, and being unable to hold ourselves above it or apart from it." (page 94)

- In which aspect(s) of community life and society do you most long to see change?

- Identify some things you could do to meaningfully engage in this issue, to make it "your concern." This could start with educating yourself more about the issue or finding and listening deeply to people negatively impacted by the issue.

- Notice what arises in you as you contemplate moving forward in these ways.

- What thoughts, feelings, or sensations do you experience?

- Decide on one action you can take in the next week.

EIGHT

Doing and Saying

1. Reflection

Read the following lines and reflect on the questions contained within the quote:

> "But have you ever noticed the huge leap the creed makes between 'born of the Virgin Mary' and 'suffered under Pontius Pilate'? *A single comma* connects the two statements, and falling into that yawning gap, as if it were a mere detail, is *everything* Jesus said and did between his birth and his death! Called the 'Great Comma,' this gap certainly invites some serious questions. Did all the things Jesus said and did in those years not count for much? Were they nothing to 'believe' in? Was it only his birth and death that mattered? Does the gap in some way explain Christianity's often dismal record of imitating Jesus's actual life and teaching?" (pages 103–104)

- ▸ Take some time to respond in your journal to each question in the quote.

2. Reflection

> "You wouldn't guess this from the official creeds, but after all is said and done, doing is more important than saying. Jesus was clearly more concerned with what Buddhists call 'right action' ('orthopraxy' in Christianity) than with right saying, or even right thinking. You can hear this message very clearly in his parable of the two sons in Matthew 21:28–31: One son says he won't work in the vineyard, but then does, while the other says he will go, but in fact doesn't. Jesus told his listeners that he preferred the one who actually goes although saying the wrong words, over the one who says the right words but does not act. How did we miss that?" (pages 106–107)

▸ Which of these two approaches has most characterized your experience of religion today—is it focused on right action (orthopraxy) or right saying (orthodoxy)? How has this impacted what you focus on in your life?

3. Contemplative Sit

Leading in with the quotation below, practice a contemplative sit. You may wish to set a timer or digital prayer bell for 10, 15, or 20 minutes, so that you know when to finish.

Seat yourself in a quiet area. Once you are settled, read the passage aloud—this is the opening text for your sit:

> "Humanity now needs a Jesus who is historical, relevant for real life, physical and concrete, like we are. A Jesus whose life can save you even more than his death. A Jesus we can practically imitate, and who sets the bar for what it means to be fully human. And a Christ who is big enough to hold all creation together in one harmonious unity." (page 107)

- Notice any tightness in your shoulders and neck and allow any tension in your muscles to relax.

- Allow your back to rest in an aligned, neutral position.

- Ground yourself and allow your breathing to settle. Then read the following aloud, pausing between each sentence:

"I am not trying to 'achieve' anything. There are no goals. I am simply becoming aware of this moment. Becoming aware of my presence in this moment. As I notice any distractions, thoughts, judgments, decisions, ideas that cross my mind, I let them go for now, focusing instead on my moment-by-moment experience of being present to What Is. God's Presence. The Larger Field. *En Cristo.*

"As I become distracted, frustrated, or confused, I consciously return to offering my moment-by-moment presence to God's Presence. God's Presence is already within me, whether I'm aware of it or not. No offering up is needed—I am offering in. Into the silence. Into each moment that I sit in contemplation.

"Christ . . . is big enough to hold all creation together in one harmonious unity." [Pause]

- Ring a prayer bell to indicate that the contemplative sit has begun.

Silence for 10, 15, or 20 minutes

Once the closing prayer bell or timer sounds, briefly write down what this experience was like for you.

4. *Lectio* **Practice**

> "In Franciscan theology, *truth is always for the sake of love—and not an absolute end in itself, which too often becomes the worship of an ideology.* In other words, any good idea that does not engage the body, the heart, the physical world, and the people around us will tend to be more theological problem solving and theory than any real healing of people and institutions—which ironically is about all Jesus does!" (page 106)

Read the above quotation a couple of times before moving on to the text below for the *Lectio* reflection.

> *"Truth is always for the sake of love."*

1. With the first reading, allow yourself to *settle in* to the exercise and familiarize yourself with the words. Read the text out loud, very slowly and clearly. Pause for a breath or two before moving on.

2. For the second reading, *listen* from a centered heart space and notice any word or phrase that stands out to you.

3. After a few moments of silence, read the text a third time, *reflecting* on how this word or phrase is connected to your current life experience. Take a minute to linger over this word or phrase, "to focus on it until it engages your body, your heart, your awareness of the physical [and unseen] world around you." (page 8)

   You may want to speak a response aloud or write something in your journal.

4. For the final reading, *respond* with a prayer or expression of what you have experienced, inviting the infinite wisdom of God to support you in places of unknowing, confusion, desire, or hope.

Allow the text to sink in and settle within your whole being before moving on.

5. Creative Reflection

> "There are other glaring oversights in the creeds. Believed to be the earliest formal declaration of Christian belief, the Apostles' Creed does not once mention love, service, hope, the 'least of the brothers and sisters,' or even forgiveness—anything, actually, that is remotely *actionable*. . . . Both [the Apostles' and Nicene] creeds reveal historic Christian assumptions about who God is and what God is doing. They reaffirm a static and unchanging universe, and a God who is quite remote from almost everything we care about each day. Furthermore, they don't show much interest in the realities of Jesus's own human life—or ours. Instead, they portray what religious systems tend to want: a God who looks strong and stable and in control." (page 104)

Select a creed: the Apostles' Creed, the Nicene Creed, or any of the dozens of other ecumenical and denominational creeds (many of these can easily be found online).

- Read over the creed several times, then answer the following questions:
  - With which lines do you most connect?
  - With which lines do you struggle to connect?
  - What's missing for you?
- Write a line, a journal entry, or even a poem about what else is coming up for you right now.

NINE

Things at Their Depth

1. Reflection

"As I watch Catholics receive communion at Mass, I notice that some, after taking the bread and wine, turn toward the altar or the sacred box that reserves the bread and bow or genuflect as a gesture of respect—as if the Presence were still over there. In those moments, I wonder if they have missed what just happened! Don't they realize that the Eucharist was supposed to be a full transference of identity *to them?*" (page 109)

"Likewise, I have known many Evangelicals who 'received Jesus into their hearts' but still felt the need to 'get saved' again every Friday night. Did they not believe that a real transformation happened if they made a genuine surrender and reconnected to their Source? Most of us understandably start the journey assuming that God is 'up there,' and our job is to transcend this world to find 'him.' We spend so much time trying to get 'up there,' we miss that God's big leap in Jesus was to come 'down here.' So much of our worship and religious effort is the spiritual equivalent of trying to go up what has become the down escalator." (page 110)

- ► What experiences of focusing on getting "up there" have shaped your faith and spirituality in the past?
- ► At this point in your life, would you say you are more focused on getting "up there" to connect with God or allowing God to come "down here" as "a full transference of identity" *to you*? Describe what that's like.

2. Reflection

"Knowing and loving Jesus is largely about becoming fully human, wounds and all, instead of ascending spiritually or thinking we can remain unwounded. (The ego does not like this fundamental switch at all, so we keep returning to some kind of performance principle, trying to climb out of this messy incarnation instead of learning from it. This is most early-stage religion.)" (page 110)

- ► Where might you be invited to become more human right now?
- ► What wounds do you need to accept as part of this journey of descending rather than ascending?
- ► What are you currently learning from "this messy incarnation"?

"Jesus invited Thomas and all doubters into a *tangible* kind of religion, a religion that makes touching human pain and suffering the way into both compassion and understanding." (page 113)

"Our central message again bears repeating: *God loves things by becoming them. We love God by continuing the same pattern.*" (page 113)

- In what aspect of your life is this pattern of "becoming" most tangible?

3. *Lectio* Practice

> "Throughout his life, Jesus himself spent no time climbing, but a lot of time descending, *'emptying himself and becoming as all humans are'* (Philippians 2:7)." (page 110)

1. With the first reading, allow yourself to *settle in* to the exercise and familiarize yourself with the words. Read the text out loud, very slowly and clearly. Pause for a breath or two before moving on.

2. For the second reading, *listen* from a centered heart space and notice any word or phrase that stands out to you.

3. After a few moments of silence, read the text a third time, *reflecting* on how this word or phrase is connected to your current life experience. Take a minute to linger over this word or phrase, "to focus on it until it engages your body, your heart, your awareness of the physical [and unseen] world around you." (page 8)

    You may want to speak a response aloud or write something in your journal.

4. For the final reading, *respond* with a prayer or expression of what you have experienced, inviting the infinite wisdom of God to support you in places of unknowing, confusion, desire, or hope.

    Allow the text to sink in and settle within your whole being before moving on.

4. Reflection

"St. Bonaventure (1221–1274) taught that, 'As a human being Christ has something in common with all creatures. . . .' Bonaventure was trying to give theological weight to the deep experience of St. Francis of Assisi (1181–1226), who . . . [called] animals and elements and even the forces of nature by familial names: 'Sister, Mother Earth,' 'Brother Wind,' 'Sister Water,' and 'Brother Fire.'" (page 112)

"In his book *Unmasking the Powers* theologian and biblical scholar Walter Wink makes a very convincing case that this intuition about the inherent sacredness of creation is precisely what sacred texts are pointing toward when they speak of 'angels.' An angel, Wink believed, is *the inner spirit or soul of a thing.* When we honor the 'angel' or soul of a thing, we respect its inner spirit. And if we learn how to pay attention to the soul of things—to see the 'angels' of elements, animals, the earth, water, and skies—then we can naturally work our way back through the Great Chain of Being to the final link, whom many call God." (page 117)

Think of a person (or a natural element or an animal) with whom you find it difficult to engage.

- ► Which aspects of their inner spirit/soul/"angel" have you been ignoring or distorting? Be honest with yourself and consider aspects of their inner soul that you may be resisting. (Take some time over this, perhaps journaling, drawing, or engaging in some kind of creative process as you reflect.)

- ► How can you respect this inner spirit/soul/"angel" and, in turn, their whole being?

5. Contemplative Sit

Leading in with the quotations below, practice a contemplative sit. You may wish to set a timer or digital prayer bell for 10, 15, or 20 minutes, so that you know when to finish.

Seat yourself in a quiet area. Once you are settled, read the passage aloud—this is the opening text for your sit:

> "If you think I am emphasizing the experiential too much, just remember that both Jesus and Paul trusted their own experience of God against the status quo of their own Jewish religion." (page 116)

> "Today we have freedom and permission and the tools to move toward depth as few people ever had in human history. What a shame it would be if we did not use them. The best way *out* is if we have first gone *in*. The only way we can trust *up* is if we have gone *down*." (page 115)

> "What I am saying in this chapter is that there must be a way to be both *here* and in the *depth of here*. Jesus is the here, Christ is the depth of here." (page 118)

- ▸ Notice any tightness in your shoulders and neck and allow any tension in your muscles to relax.

- ▸ Allow your back to rest in an aligned, neutral position.

- ▸ Ground yourself and allow your breathing to settle. Then read the following aloud, pausing between each sentence:

> "I am not trying to 'achieve' anything. There are no goals. I am simply becoming aware of this moment. Becoming aware of my presence in this moment. As I notice any distractions, thoughts,

judgments, decisions, ideas that cross my mind, I let them go for now, focusing instead on my moment-by-moment experience of being present to What Is. God's Presence. The Larger Field. *En Cristo*.

"As I become distracted, frustrated, or confused, I consciously return to offering my moment-by-moment presence to God's Presence. God's Presence is already within me, whether I'm aware of it or not. No offering up is needed—I am offering in. Into the silence. Into each moment that I sit in contemplation.

"There must be a way to be both *here* and in the *depth of here*. Jesus is the here, Christ is the depth of here." [Pause]

▸ Ring a prayer bell to indicate that the contemplative sit has begun.

Silence for 10, 15, or 20 minutes

Once the closing prayer bell or timer sounds, briefly write down what this experience was like for you.

6. Reflection

"*God hides in the depths and is not seen as long as we stay on the surface of anything—even the depths of our sins.* Remember, the archetypal encounter between doubting Thomas and the Risen Jesus (John 20:19–28) is not really a story about believing in the fact of the resurrection, but a story about believing that someone could *be wounded and also resurrected at the same time!* That is a quite different message, and still desperately needed. 'Put your finger here,' Jesus says to Thomas (20:27). And, like Thomas, we are indeed wounded and resurrected at the same time, all of us. In fact, this might be the primary pastoral message of the whole Gospel." (page 111)

Slowly read over the above quotation several times.

- Notice what you are drawn toward. Which word or phrase most speaks to you?
- Take a couple of minutes to write down anything that this word or phrase evokes within you.

7. Reflection

"I doubt if you can see the image of God *(Imago Dei)* in your fellow humans if you cannot first see it in rudimentary form in stones, in plants and flowers, in strange little animals, in bread and wine, and most especially cannot honor this objective divine image in yourself. It is a full-body tune-up, this spiritual journey. It really ends up being *all or nothing, here and then everywhere.*" (page 119)

"*What you choose now, you shall have later* seems to be the realization of the saints. Not an idyllic hope for a later heaven but a living experience right now. We cannot jump over this world, or its woundedness, and still try to love God. We must love God *through, in, with,* and even *because of* this world. This is the message Christianity was supposed to initiate, proclaim, and encourage, and what Jesus modeled. We were made to love and trust this world, 'to cultivate it and take care of it' (Genesis 2:15)." (pages 112–113)

- In what ways do you naturally "cultivate and take care of" the world in which you live? (This can be related to people, nature, or anything else.)

Reflect on a time when you engaged in one of these cultivating activities.

- How did you feel while you were engaging in these loving activities?
- What impact did it have on you afterward?

8. Reflection

"We all know *respect* when we see it (re-spect = to see a second time). We all know reverence because it softens our gaze. *Any object that calls forth respect or reverence is the 'Christ' or the anointed one for us at that moment.*" (page 119)

"All people who see with that second kind of contemplative gaze, all who look at the world with respect, even if they are not formally religious, are *en Cristo*, or in Christ. For them, as Thomas Merton says, 'the gate of heaven is everywhere' because of their freedom to respect what is right in front of them—all the time." (page 120)

- What objects are calling forth a heartfelt respect and reverence in you at this moment?

Spend a couple of minutes noticing what it is you respect and revere.

9. Engage

"Humanity has grown tired of grand, overarching societal plans like communism and Nazism, and of disembodied spiritualities that allow no validation or verification in experience. Too often they hide an agenda of power and control, obfuscating and distracting us from what is right in front of us. This is exactly what we do when we make the emphasis of Jesus's Gospel what is 'out there' as opposed to what is 'in here.' For example, insisting on a literal belief in the virgin birth of Jesus is very good theological symbolism, but unless it translates into a spirituality of interior poverty, readiness to conceive, and human vulnerability, it is largely a 'mere lesson memorized' as Isaiah puts it (29:13). It 'saves' no one. Likewise, an intellectual belief that Jesus rose from the dead is a good start, but until you are struck by the realization that the crucified and risen Jesus is a parable about the journey of all humans, and even the universe, it is a rather harmless—if not harmful—belief that will leave you and the world largely unchanged." (page 114)

- Take a moment to reflect on Mary's spirituality of interior poverty, readiness to conceive, and human vulnerability.

- Drawing from your own spiritual experience, in what ways have you responded to God in similar ways?

- What would it mean for your approach to your spirituality to be "struck by the realization that the crucified and risen Jesus is a parable about the journey of all humans, and even the universe"?

- How might you engage differently in the world?

TEN

The Feminine Incarnation

"The Mary symbol brought together the two disparate worlds of matter and spirit, feminine mother and masculine child, earth and heaven, whether we like it or not." (page 126)

1. Contemplative Sit

Leading in with the quotation below, practice a contemplative sit. You may wish to set a timer or digital prayer bell for 10, 15, or 20 minutes, so that you know when to finish.

Seat yourself in a quiet area. Once you are settled, read the passage aloud—this is the opening text for your sit:

> "The first incarnation (creation) is symbolized by Sophia-Incarnate, a beautiful, feminine, multicolored, graceful Mary.

> "She is invariably offering us Jesus, God incarnated into vulnerability and nakedness.

"Mary became the Symbol of the First Universal Incarnation.

"She then hands the Second Incarnation on to us, while remaining in the background; the focus is always on the child.

"Earth Mother presenting Spiritual Son, the two first stages of the Incarnation.

"Feminine Receptivity, handing on the fruit of her yes.

"And inviting us to offer our own yes." (pages 123–124)

▸ Notice any tightness in your shoulders and neck and allow any tension in your muscles to relax.

▸ Allow your back to rest in an aligned, neutral position.

▸ Ground yourself and allow your breathing to settle. Then read the following aloud, pausing between each sentence:

"I am not trying to 'achieve' anything. There are no goals. I am simply becoming aware of this moment. Becoming aware of my presence in this moment. As I notice any distractions, thoughts, judgments, decisions, ideas that cross my mind, I let them go for now, focusing instead on my moment-by-moment experience of being present to What Is. God's Presence. The Larger Field. *En Cristo*.

"As I become distracted, frustrated, or confused, I consciously return to offering my moment-by-moment presence to God's Presence. God's Presence is already within me, whether I'm aware of it or not. No offering up is needed—I am offering in. Into the silence. Into each moment that I sit in contemplation.

"Earth Mother presenting Spiritual Son, the two first stages of the Incarnation.

"Feminine Receptivity, handing on the fruit of her yes.
And inviting us to offer our own yes." [Pause]

- Ring a prayer bell to indicate that the contemplative sit has begun.

Silence for 10, 15, or 20 minutes

Once the closing prayer bell or timer sounds, briefly write down what this experience was like for you.

2. Reflection

"Jung believed that humans produce in art *the inner images the soul needs in order to see itself and to allow its own transformation.*" (page 123)

"In the mythic imagination, I think Mary intuitively symbolizes the first Incarnation—or Mother Earth, if you will allow me. (I am not saying Mary *is* the first incarnation, only that she became the natural archetype and symbol for it, particularly in art, which is perhaps why the Madonna is still the most painted subject in Western art.) I believe that Mary is the major feminine archetype for the Christ Mystery. This archetype had already shown herself as *Sophia* or Holy Wisdom (see Proverbs 8:1ff., Wisdom 7:7ff.), and again in the book of Revelation (12:1–17) in the cosmic symbol of 'a Woman clothed with the sun and standing on the moon.' Neither Sophia nor the Woman of Revelation is precisely Mary of Nazareth, yet in so many ways, both are—and each broadens our understanding of the Divine Feminine." (page 123)

- Take a couple of minutes to read over the above quotations a few times. What comes up for you?
- How does the idea that "Mary is the major feminine archetype for the Christ Mystery" sit with you?

3. Reflection

"But by the time of the much-needed Protestant Reformation, all we could see was 'but she is not God.' Which is entirely true. But we could no longer see in wholes, and see that even better, 'She is us!' That is why we loved her, probably without fully understanding why. (Much of the human race can more easily imagine unconditional love coming from the feminine and the maternal more than from a man.) I have to say this!

"In the many images of Mary, humans see our own feminine soul. We needed to see ourselves in her, and say with her 'God has looked upon me in my lowliness. From now on, all generations will call me blessed' (Luke 1:48).

"I do realize the dangers here, and I acknowledge that for all practical purposes many Catholics divinized Mary, probably out of sentimentality. All the same, I invite you to consider the deeper and more subtle message. I have often said that many Catholics have a poor theology of Mary but an excellent psychology: *Humans like, need, and trust our mothers to give us gifts, to nurture us, and always to forgive us, which is what we want from God.*" (pages 124–125)

▸ Reflect on your childhood, your relationship with your mother, and, if it applies, your experiences of motherhood. How do these experiences affect the way you relate to Mary?

4. Reflection

"We are clearly dealing with not just a single woman here but a foundational symbol—or, to borrow the language of Carl Jung, an 'archetype'—an image that constellates a whole host of meanings that cannot be communicated logically. Nothing emerges that broadly and over so much of time if it is not grounded somehow in our collective human unconscious. One would be foolish to dismiss such things lightly." (page 123)

"Although Jesus was clearly of the masculine gender, the Christ is beyond gender, and so it should be expected that the Big Tradition would have found feminine ways, consciously or unconsciously, to symbolize the full Divine Incarnation and to give God a more feminine character—as the Bible itself often does." (page 122)

- ▸ What resonates from these quotations?
- ▸ Is there anything that you find challenging or confusing?

5. *Lectio* **Practice**

"In the many images of Mary, humans see our own feminine soul. We needed to see ourselves in her, and say with her 'God has looked upon me in my lowliness. From now on, all generations will call me blessed' (Luke 1:48)." (page 124)

1. With the first reading, allow yourself to *settle in* to the exercise and familiarize yourself with the words. Read the text out loud, very slowly and clearly. Pause for a breath or two before moving on.

2. For the second reading, *listen* from a centered heart space and notice any word or phrase that stands out to you.

3. After a few moments of silence, read the text a third time, *reflecting* on how this word or phrase is connected to your current life experience. Take a minute to linger over this word or phrase, "to focus on it until it engages your body, your heart, your awareness of the physical [and unseen] world around you." (page 8)

You may want to speak a response aloud or write something in your journal.

4.   For the final reading, *respond* with a prayer or expression of what you have experienced, inviting the infinite wisdom of God to support you in places of unknowing, confusion, desire, or hope.

Allow the text to sink in and settle within your whole being before moving on.

6. Reflection

"My years of work with men's groups have convinced me . . . [that] the more macho and patriarchal a culture, the greater its devotion to Mary. I once counted eleven images of Mary in a single Catholic church in Texas cowboy country. I see that as a culture trying unconsciously, and often not very successfully, to balance itself out. In the same way, Mary gives women in the Catholic church a dominant feminine image to counterbalance all the males parading around up front!" (page 125)

"We always had the feminine incarnation, in fact it was the first incarnation, and even better, it moved toward including all of us! *Mary is all of us* both *receiving and handing on the gift.* We liked her precisely because she was one of us—and *not* God! I think Christians of the first thousand years understood this on an intuitive and allegorical level." (page 124)

Notice the emotions and the sensations you feel in your body right now (you may want to read over the quotations once more).

"Mary is all of us both *receiving and handing on the gift."*

- What does this line evoke within you?
- In what ways do you receive the gift?
- In what ways do you hand on the gift?

7. Reflection

"The point is that in some ways, many humans can identify with Mary more than they can with Jesus precisely because she was *not* God, but the archetype for our yes to God!" (page 127)

"In Mary, humanity has said *our* eternal yes to God.

"A yes that cannot be undone.

"A corporate yes that overrides our many noes.

"This is why Mary was commonly called the 'New Eve,' who undid the corporate no of the first Eve, and is invariably pictured in art stepping on the snake that tempted Eve (Genesis 3:15)." (page 128)

"Mary is the Great Yes that humanity forever needs for Christ to be born into the world." (page 127)

- In what ways are you currently being invited to give your "Great Yes" for Christ to be born into the world?

8. Reflection

"Like the Christ Mystery itself, *the deep feminine* often works underground and in the shadows, and—from that position—creates a much more intoxicating message." (page 128)

"Today on many levels, we are witnessing an immense longing for the mature feminine at every level of our society—from our politics, to our economics, in our psyche, our cultures, our patterns of leadership, and our theologies, all of which have become far too warlike, competitive, mechanistic, and noncontemplative. We are terribly imbalanced." (page 128)

Perhaps giving our Great Yes to Christ is a call to working "underground and in the shadows," creating "a much more intoxicating message."

- In which aspects of society do you feel the longing for the mature feminine?
- What would it be like for you to engage "underground and in the shadows" to bring some balance to that aspect of society?

Notice any part of your ego that resists this idea and become open to the resistance, staying with it until it calms. Remember, *how you do anything is how you do everything.*" (page 57)

ELEVEN

This Is My Body

"'Life is the destiny you are bound to refuse until you have consented to die.'"
—W. H. Auden, "For the Time Being" (page 129)

1. Reflection

"I realized that Jesus did not say, 'This is my spirit, given for you,' or even 'These are my thoughts.' Instead, he very daringly said, 'This is my *body*,' which seems like an overly physical and risky way for a spiritual teacher, a God-man, to speak. . . . In offering his body, *Jesus is precisely giving us his full bodily humanity more than his spiritualized divinity!* 'Eat me,' he shockingly says, eating being such a fundamental bodily action, more basic and primitive than thinking or talking." (page 130)

"Much of ancient religion portrayed God eating or sacrificing humans or animals, which were offered on the altars, but Jesus turned religion and history on their heads, inviting us to imagine that God would give *himself as food for us!*" (pages 130–131)

"This 'water and blood' had always struck me as strange symbolism. But maybe not for a woman, who knows the price of birth. How daring and shocking it was for Jesus to turn the whole tradition of impure blood on its heels and make blood *holy*—and even a point of contact with the divine!" (page 135)

- ▸ Which aspects of these quotations do you find most striking? Take some time to reflect and let them sink in.

2. Reflection

"When Jesus spoke the words 'This is my Body,' I believe he was speaking not just about the bread right in front of him, but about the whole universe, about every thing that is physical, material, and yet also spirit-filled. . . . His assertion and our repetition resound over all creation before they also settle into one piece of bread. And you know what? The bread and wine, and all of creation, seem to believe who and what they are much more readily than humans do." (pages 131–132)

- ▸ How do these understandings of "'This is my *body*'" compare to what you have heard or thought before?

Take a moment to read over the final sentence one more time.

- ▸ How do you hear this today?
- ▸ To what extent is this relevant in your life?

3. Reflection

"Merely assenting to or saying the words will never give us the jolt we need *to absorb the divine desire for us—and for Itself.* Frankly, we're talking about the difference between receiving a sincere Valentine's Day card that says, 'I love you,' and making physical, naked, and tender love to someone you deeply care about and who cares for you. Why are we so afraid of that?" (pages 136–137)

"This is why I must hold to the orthodox belief that there is Real Presence in the bread and wine. For me, *if we sacrifice Reality in the elements, we end up sacrificing the same Reality in ourselves.* As Flannery O'Connor once declared: 'Well, if it is just a symbol, to hell with it!'" (page 137)

- ▸ With which aspects of the above quotations do you most resonate?
- ▸ What doesn't sit so well with you?

Write down any reflections you have from experiencing these feelings of comfort and discomfort.

4. Contemplative Sit

Leading in with the quotation below, practice a contemplative sit. You may wish to set a timer or digital prayer bell for 10, 15, or 20 minutes, so that you know when to finish.

Seat yourself in a quiet area. Once you are settled, read the passage aloud—this is the opening text for your sit:

"It seems that mere mind-knowing is not enough, because it does not engage the heart or soul. The mistake happens when those who cannot make this mental assent are deemed 'unworthy' to receive. But your only real prerequisite for participation or 'worthiness' is in fact *your capacity for presence* yourself. This is not accomplished just in the head. Presence is a unique capacity that includes body, heart, mind, and whatever we mean by 'soul.' Love affairs never happen just in the mind.

"Only presence can know presence. And our real presence can know Real Presence." (page 131)

▸ Notice any tightness in your shoulders and neck and allow any tension in your muscles to relax.

▸ Allow your back to rest in an aligned, neutral position.

▸ Ground yourself and allow your breathing to settle. Then read the following aloud, pausing between each sentence:

"I am not trying to 'achieve' anything. There are no goals. I am simply becoming aware of this moment. Becoming aware of my presence in this moment. As I notice any distractions, thoughts, judgments, decisions, ideas that cross my mind, I let them go for now, focusing instead on my moment-by-moment experience of being present to What Is. God's Presence. The Larger Field. *En Cristo.*

"As I become distracted, frustrated, or confused, I consciously return to offering my moment-by-moment presence to God's Presence. God's Presence is already within me, whether I'm aware of it or not. No offering up is needed—I am offering in. Into the silence. Into each moment that I sit in contemplation.

"Only presence can know presence. And our real presence can know Real Presence." [Pause]

▸ Ring a prayer bell to indicate that the contemplative sit has begun.

Silence for 10, 15, or 20 minutes

Once the closing prayer bell or timer sounds, briefly write down what this experience was like for you.

5. Memories

> "One of the things I've learned from studying male initiation rites is that startling, vivid rituals are the only ones that have much psychic effect—things like symbolic drowning, digging your own grave, rolling naked in ashes. . . . There's a real difference between harmless repetitive ceremonies and life-changing rituals. *Scholars say that ceremonies normally confirm and celebrate the status quo and deny the shadow side of things (think of a Fourth of July parade), whereas true ritual offers an alternative universe, where the shadow is named (think of a true Eucharist). In the church, I am afraid we mostly have ceremonies.*" (page 133)

- ► What are the most memorable ceremonies in which you have participated?
- ► What are the most memorable rituals in which you have participated?
- ► What has been the difference?
- ► Into which category would you place the Eucharistic meal?
- ► What depth of impact has the Eucharist had on you?

6. *Lectio* Practice

Read the following quotation a couple of times before moving on to the *Lectio* reflection:

> "Eucharist is the Incarnation of Christ taken to its final shape and end—the very elements of the earth itself.

"It is all one continuum of Incarnation.

"*Who we are in God is who we all are.*

"Everything else is changing and passing away." (page 138)

1. With the first reading, allow yourself to *settle in* to the exercise and familiarize yourself with the words. Read the text out loud, very slowly and clearly. Pause for a breath or two before moving on.

2. For the second reading, *listen* from a centered heart space and notice any word or phrase that stands out to you.

3. After a few moments of silence, read the text a third time, *reflecting* on how this word or phrase is connected to your current life experience. Take a minute to linger over this word or phrase, "to focus on it until it engages your body, your heart, your awareness of the physical [and unseen] world around you." (page 8)

   You may want to speak a response aloud or write something in your journal.

4. For the final reading, *respond* with a prayer or expression of what you have experienced, inviting the infinite wisdom of God to support you in places of unknowing, confusion, desire, or hope.

   Allow the text to sink in and settle within your whole being before moving on.

7. Engage

"Many mystics and liberation theologians have further recognized that inviting us to drink wine *as his blood* is an invitation to live in bodily solidarity 'with the blood of every person whose blood has been unjustly shed on this earth, from the blood of Abel the Holy to the blood of Zechariah' (Matthew 23:35)." (page 133)

- ▸ Take a minute to reflect upon the injustice in our world.
- ▸ Drinking the wine "*as his blood*," what is *your* "invitation to live in bodily solidarity" with those who suffer?
- ▸ What does this inspire you to do?

8. Reflection

"We are not just humans having a God experience. The Eucharist tells us that, in some mysterious way, we are God having a human experience!

"This continues in Romans 8:18–25 (as creation), 1 Corinthians 10:16ff. and 11:23ff. (as bread and wine), and in 12:12ff. (as people). In each of these Scriptures, and in an ever-expanding sense, Paul expresses his full belief that there is a real transfer of human and spiritual identity from Christ to Creation, to the elements of bread and wine, and through them to human beings. The Great Circle of Inclusion (the Trinity) is a centrifugal force that will finally pull everything back into itself—exactly as many physicists predict will happen to the universe the moment it finally stops expanding. They call it the 'Big Crunch,' and some even say it will take a nano-second to happen. (Could this be a real description of the 'Second Coming of Christ'? Or the 'Final Judgment'? I think so.)" (page 137)

- ▸ What does it mean to you to be part of this "Great Circle of Inclusion"?

- Where are you expanding this Great Circle in your life, your family, your community?

TWELVE

Why Did Jesus Die?

1. Reflection

"Thinking he could solve the problem of sin inside of the medieval code of feudal honor and shame, Anselm said, in effect, 'Yes, a price did need to be paid to restore God's honor, and it needed to be paid to God the Father—by one who was equally divine.' . . . In authoritarian and patriarchal cultures, most people were fully programmed to think this way. . . . This understanding also nullifies any in-depth spiritual journey: *Why would you love or trust or desire to be with such a God?*" (page 143)

"Over the next few centuries, Anselm's honor- and shame-based way of thinking came to be accepted among Christians, though it met resistance from some, particularly my own Franciscan school. Protestants accepted the mainline Catholic position, and embraced it with even more fervor. Evangelicals later enshrined it as one of the 'four pillars' of foundational Christian belief, which the earlier period would have thought strange." (page 143)

- As you read these quotations, did you primarily focus on the ideas and theology or your personal experience of shame-based thinking? Notice any thoughts and emotions that arise within you as you reflect.

- What memories do you have of when you engaged with this topic in the past?

- What is your experience now?

2. Contemplative Sit

Leading in with the quotation below, practice a contemplative sit. You may wish to set a timer or digital prayer bell for 10, 15, or 20 minutes, so that you know when to finish.

Seat yourself in a quiet area. Once you are settled, read the passages aloud—these are the opening texts for your sit:

> "Love cannot be bought by some 'necessary sacrifice'; if it could, it would not and could not work its transformative effects. Try loving your spouse or children that way, and see where it gets you." (page 144)

> "John Duns Scotus (1266–1308), refused to see the Incarnation, and its final denouement on the cross, as a mere reaction to sin. Instead, [he and the Franciscans] claimed that the cross was a *freely chosen revelation of Total Love* on God's part." (page 143)

- Notice any tightness in your shoulders and neck and allow any tension in your muscles to relax.

- Allow your back to rest in an aligned, neutral position.

- Ground yourself and allow your breathing to settle. Then read the following aloud, pausing between each sentence:

"I am not trying to 'achieve' anything. There are no goals. I am simply becoming aware of this moment. Becoming aware of my presence in this moment. As I notice any distractions, thoughts, judgments, decisions, ideas that cross my mind, I let them go for now, focusing instead on my moment-by-moment experience of being present to What Is. God's Presence. The Larger Field. *En Cristo*.

"As I become distracted, frustrated, or confused, I consciously return to offering my moment-by-moment presence to God's Presence. God's Presence is already within me, whether I'm aware of it or not. No offering up is needed—I am offering in. Into the silence. Into each moment that I sit in contemplation.

"The cross was a *freely chosen revelation of Total Love* on God's part." [Pause]

➤ Ring a prayer bell to indicate that the contemplative sit has begun.

Silence for 10, 15, or 20 minutes

Once the closing prayer bell or timer sounds, briefly write down what this experience was like for you.

3. Reflection

*"It is not God who is violent. We are.
It is not that God demands suffering of humans. We do.
God does not need or want suffering—neither in Jesus nor in us."* (page 146)

➤ Sit with this quotation for one minute, then record anything that comes up for you in your journal.

4. Reflection

> "Most of us are still programmed to read the Scriptures according to the common laws of jurisprudence, which are hardly ever based on *restorative justice*. . . . Restorative justice was the amazing discovery of the Jewish prophets, in which Yahweh punished Israel by loving them even more! (Ezekiel 16:53ff.)" (page 146)

‣ What has been your experience of God's restorative justice?

5. Reflection

As you read through the following quotations, notice what resonates with you:

> "The Divine Mind transforms all human suffering by identifying completely with the human predicament and standing in full solidarity with it from beginning to end. This is the real meaning of the crucifixion. The cross is not just a singular event. It's a statement from God that *reality has a cruciform pattern*." (page 147)

> "'There is a science about which God knows nothing—addition and subtraction.'" (Thérèse of Lisieux, paraphrase, page 147)

> "If we do not recognize that we ourselves are the problem, we will continue to make God the scapegoat—which is exactly what we did by the killing of the God-Man on the cross. The crucifixion of Jesus—whom we see as the Son of God—was a devastating prophecy that humans would sooner kill God than change themselves. Yet the God-Man suffers our rejection willingly so something bigger can happen." (page 154)

‣ Read over the quotations one more time. What strikes you now?

6. *Lectio* **Practice**

"He did not come to change God's mind about us. It did not need changing. Jesus came to change our minds about God—and about ourselves—and about where goodness and evil really lie." (page 151)

1. With the first reading, allow yourself to *settle in* to the exercise and familiarize yourself with the words. Read the text out loud, very slowly and clearly. Pause for a breath or two before moving on.

2. For the second reading, *listen* from a centered heart space and notice any word or phrase that stands out to you.

3. After a few moments of silence, read the text a third time, *reflecting* on how this word or phrase is connected to your current life experience. Take a minute to linger over this word or phrase, "to focus on it until it engages your body, your heart, your awareness of the physical [and unseen] world around you." (page 8)

   You may want to speak a response aloud or write something in your journal.

4. For the final reading, *respond* with a prayer or expression of what you have experienced, inviting the infinite wisdom of God to support you in places of unknowing, confusion, desire, or hope.

   Allow the text to sink in and settle within your whole being before moving on.

7. Reflection

"A transformative religion must touch us at this primitive, brain-stem level, or it is not transformative at all. History is continually graced with people who somehow learned to act beyond and outside their self-interest and for the good of the world, people who clearly operated by a power larger than their own. . . . I can't say how one becomes such a person. All I can presume is that they all had their Christ moments, in which they stopped denying their own shadows, stopped projecting those shadows elsewhere, and agreed to own their deepest identity in solidarity with the world." (page 152)

Take a moment to read through this quotation one more time.

Then write down, for one minute each, your thoughts on the following:

- ▸ Your own Christ moment
- ▸ Your own shadow
- ▸ Your sense of solidarity with the world at this point in time

8. Engage

"Saints are those who wake up while in this world, instead of waiting for the next one. Francis of Assisi, William Wilberforce, Thérèse of Lisieux, and Harriet Tubman did not feel superior to anyone else; they just knew they had been let in on a big divine secret, and they wanted to do their part in revealing it.

"*They all refused to trust even their own power unless that power had first been taught and refined by powerlessness.*

"This is no easy truth. Once their entire frame of mind had been taken apart and reshaped in this way, they had to figure out how they fit back into the dominant worldview—and most of them never did, at least not completely. This became their crucifixion. The 'way of the cross' can never go out of style because it will surely never be *in* style. It never becomes the dominant consciousness anywhere. But this is the powerlessness of God, the powerlessness that saves the world." (page 153)

- What resonates with you?
- What do you shy away from?
- How do these quotations impact the manner in which you engage with:
  - family?
  - friends?
  - neighbors?

- How do these quotations impact your engagement:
  - in your local community (e.g., community work)?
  - in the country where you live (e.g., racial inequality, people trafficking, advocacy)?
  - as a global citizen (e.g., environmental movements)?

9. Meditation: "A Dialogue with the Crucified God"

"Wait until you have an open, quiet, and solitary slot of time, then pray it out loud so your ears can hear your own words from your own mouth. In addition, I suggest that you place yourself before a tender image of the crucified Jesus that will allow you to both give and receive." (page 155)

- Following the instructions above, read through "A Dialogue with the Crucified God" (pages 155–158), either now or at some point in the coming days.
- Journal anything that arises for you.

10. Engage

> "What the medieval mystics said is true, *Crux probat omnia*—'The cross legitimates/proves/uses everything.' *(Stay with this Christian maxim until it makes sense to you.)*" (page 158)

- "Stay with this maxim" in the days ahead and note in your journal anything that arises within you.
- Notice the cruciform pattern in your own life in the coming days. In what ways are you drawn to engage in breadth (the horizontal) and at depth (the vertical) with the world around you? Reading over your answers to Question 8 may act as a helpful prompt.

THIRTEEN

It Can't Be Carried Alone

1. Reflection

"The freeing, good news of the Gospel is that God is saving and redeeming the Whole first and foremost, and we are all caught up in this Cosmic Sweep of Divine Love. The parts—you and me and everybody else—are the blessed beneficiaries, the desperate hangers-on, the partly willing participants in the Whole. Paul wrote that our only task is to trust this reality 'until God is all in all' (1 Corinthians 15:28). What a different idea of faith! 'When Christ is revealed,' Paul writes to the Colossians, 'and he is your life—you too will be revealed in all your glory with him' (3:4). Unless and until we can enjoy this, so much of what passes for Christianity will amount to little more than well-disguised narcissism and self-referential politics. We see this phenomenon playing out in the de facto values of people who strongly identify as Christian. Often they are more racist, classist, and sexist than non-Christians. 'Others can carry the burden and the pain of injustice, but not my group,' they seem to say." (page 167)

- What is your experience of Christians who "are more racist, classist, and sexist than non-Christians," whose unconscious message is that "'others can carry the burden and the pain of injustice, but not my group'"?
- How has this been true of you?
- Reflect for a minute on the phrase, "we are all caught up in this Cosmic Sweep of Divine Love."
- How is it good news "that God is saving and redeeming the Whole first and foremost"?
- What does it mean for you?

2. Reflection

"But in those weeks before she died, Venus *somehow* communicated to me that all sadness, whether cosmic, human, or canine, is one and the same. Somehow, her eyes were all eyes, even God's eyes, and the sadness she expressed was a divine and universal sadness." (page 160)

- What life experiences have evoked particular sadness within you?
- What sadness are you carrying right now?
- Take a moment to meditate on the message of this chapter title: "It Can't Be Carried Alone."

3. Reflection

"Almost all people are carrying a great and secret hurt, even when they don't know it. When we can make the shift to realize this, it softens the space around our overly defended hearts. It makes it hard to be cruel to anyone. It somehow makes us one." (pages 161–162)

"I do believe that the only way out of deep sadness is to go *with it* and *through it*. Sometimes I wonder if this is what we mean when we lift up the chalice of wine at the Eucharist and say, 'Through him, with him, and in him.' I wonder if the only way to spiritually hold suffering—and not let it destroy us—is to recognize that we cannot do it alone. When I try to heroically do it alone, I slip into distractions, denials, and pretending—and *I do not learn suffering's softening lessons*." (page 161)

- Building on your answers to the last question, notice any:
  - distractions,
  - denials, or
  - pretending that "it's fine."

"Almost all people are carrying a great and secret hurt, even when they don't know it."

- Take some time to sit with this. You may wish to journal your reflections.
- What are *"suffering's softening lessons"* for you today?

4. Reflection

"One side effect of our individualized reading of the Gospel is that it allows the clergy great control over individual behavior, via threats and rewards. Obedience to authorities became the highest virtue in this framework, instead of love, communion, or solidarity with God or others, including the marginalized.

"We recognized hierarchical or vertical accountability but *almost no lateral accountability to one another*—as Jesus hoped for the world when he prayed that we 'all might be one' (John 17:21)." (page 165)

"I saw this in my own experience of pre–Vatican II Catholicism and seminary. In those days, I'm afraid, the only admired and promoted virtues were *obedience and loyalty to the church*. . . . Few taught us how to be the Sympathy of God or Compassion for the World, and this experience has seemed true in varying degrees in every denomination I have worked with." (pages 165–166)

- To what extent have you experienced the values of *"obedience and loyalty to the church"* being more respected than "love, communion, or solidarity with God or others, including the marginalized"?
- How did this impact you?
- Where are you most focused today?

5. Contemplative Sit

Leading in with the quotation below, practice a contemplative sit. Now that you are developing a regular practice of a contemplative sit throughout this Companion Guide, you may wish to sit for a little longer. Set a timer or digital prayer bell for 15, 20, or 25 minutes, so that you know when to finish.

Seat yourself in a quiet area. Once you are settled, read the passage aloud—this is the opening text for your sit:

"Our full 'Christ Option'—and it is indeed a free choice to jump on board—offers us so much that is both good and new—*a God who is in total solidarity with all of us at every stage of the journey, and who will get us all to our destination together in love.*

"It is no longer about being correct. It is about being connected. Being in right relationship is much, much better than just trying to be 'right.'" (page 168)

- Notice any tightness in your shoulders and neck and allow any tension in your muscles to relax.
- Allow your back to rest in an aligned, neutral position.
- Ground yourself and allow your breathing to settle. Then read the following aloud, pausing between each sentence:

"I am not trying to 'achieve' anything. There are no goals. I am simply becoming aware of this moment. Becoming aware of my presence in this moment. As I notice any distractions, thoughts, judgments, decisions, ideas that cross my mind, I let them go for now, focusing instead on my moment-by-moment experience of being present to What Is. God's Presence. The Larger Field. *En Cristo*.

"As I become distracted, frustrated, or confused, I consciously return to offering my moment-by-moment presence to God's Presence. God's Presence is already within me, whether I'm aware of it or not. No offering up is needed—I am offering in. Into the silence. Into each moment that I sit in contemplation.

"*A God who is in total solidarity with all of us at every stage of the journey, and who will get us all to our destination together in love.*

"It is no longer about being correct. It is about being connected. Being in right relationship is much, much better than just trying to be 'right.'" [Pause]

- Ring a prayer bell to indicate that the contemplative sit has begun.

Silence for 15, 20, or 25 minutes

Once the closing prayer bell or timer sounds, briefly write down what this experience was like for you.

6. Reflection

"[The author of *The Cloud of Unknowing*] reflected the more Eastern church understanding *of the resurrection as a universal phenomenon*, and not just the lone Jesus rising from the dead and raising his hands." (page 163)

"I am convinced that the Gospel offers us a holistic, 'all in one lump' understanding of things. . . . And of course, this all emerges from Jesus's major metaphor of the 'Reign of God,' a fully collective notion, which some scholars say is just about all that he talks about. Until we start reading the Jesus story through the collective notion that the Christ offers us, I honestly think we miss much of the core message, and read it all in terms of individual salvation, and individual reward and punishment. Society will remain untouched.

"I think this collective notion is what Christians were trying to verbalize when they made a late addition to the ancient Apostles' Creed, 'I believe in the communion of saints.' They were offering us this new idea that the dead are at one with the living, whether they're our direct ancestors, the saints in glory, or even the so-called souls in purgatory. The whole thing is one, just at different stages, all of it loved corporately by God (and, one hopes, by us). Within this worldview, we are saved not by being privately perfect, but by being 'part of the body,' humble links in the great chain of history." (pages 163–164)

- ▸ What does it mean to you for the core message of Christ to be the "collective notion" of the "Reign of God" rather than any individual salvation, reward, or punishment?

7. *Lectio* Practice

Read the following quotation a couple of times before moving on to the *Lectio* reflection:

> "Consider how a 'one-lump' awareness of reality upends so many of our current religious obsessions. Our arguments about private worthiness; reward and punishment; gender, race, and class distinctions; private possessions, all the things that make us argue and compete, largely become a waste of time and an illusion. All these lived arguments depend on some type of weighing, measuring, counting, listing, labeling, and comparing. The Gospel, by contrast, is about learning to live and die *in and with* God—all our warts included and forgiven by an Infinite Love. The true Gospel democratizes the world.
>
> *"We are all saved in spite of our mistakes and in spite of ourselves.*
> *We are all caught up in the cosmic sweep of Divine grace and mercy."*
> (page 166)

The text for the *Lectio* Practice is:

> *"We are all saved in spite of our mistakes and in spite of ourselves.*
> *We are all caught up in the cosmic sweep of Divine grace and mercy."*

1. With the first reading, allow yourself to *settle in* to the exercise and familiarize yourself with the words. Read the text out loud, very slowly and clearly. Pause for a breath or two before moving on.

2. For the second reading, *listen* from a centered heart space and notice any word or phrase that stands out to you.

3. After a few moments of silence, read the text a third time,

reflecting on how this word or phrase is connected to your current life experience. Take a minute to linger over this word or phrase, "to focus on it until it engages your body, your heart, your awareness of the physical [and unseen] world around you." (page 8)

You may want to speak a response aloud or write something in your journal.

4.   For the final reading, *respond* with a prayer or expression of what you have experienced, inviting the infinite wisdom of God to support you in places of unknowing, confusion, desire, or hope.

Allow the text to sink in and settle within your whole being before moving on.

8. Reflection

"I suspect that Western *individualism* has done more than any other single factor to anesthetize and even euthanize the power of the Gospel. Salvation, heaven, hell, worthiness, grace, and eternal life all came to be read through the lens of the separate ego, crowding God's transformative power out of history and society. Even Martin Luther's needed 'justification by faith' sent us on a five-hundred-year battle for the private soul of the individual. Thus leaving us with almost no care for the earth, society, the outsider, or the full Body of Christ. This is surely one reason why Christianity found itself incapable of critiquing social calamities like Nazism, slavery, and Western consumerism. For five hundred years, Christian teachers defined and redefined salvation almost entirely in individualistic terms, while well-disguised social evils—greed, pride, ambition, deceit, gluttony—moved to the highest levels of power and influence, even in our churches." (pages 164–165)

- What has been your experience of "greed, pride, ambition, deceit, gluttony" within your church?
- How would your life be affected were you to *further* shift your focus from an individual faith to one that is more focused on caring "for the earth, society, the outsider, or the full Body of Christ"?

9. Engage

"Once I know that all suffering is both *our suffering and God's suffering*, I can better endure and trust the desolations and disappointments that come my way. I can live with fewer comforts and conveniences when I see my part in global warming. I can speak with a soft and trusting voice in the public domain if doing so will help lessen human hatred and mistrust. I can stop circling the wagons around my own group, if doing so will help us recognize our common humanity.

"If I can recognize that all suffering and crucifixion (divine, planetary, human, animal) is 'one body' and will one day be transmuted into the 'one body' of cosmic resurrection (Philippians 3:21), I can at least live without going crazy or being permanently depressed. In this same passage, Paul goes on in this verse to say that 'God will do this by the same power ["operation" or "energy"] by which he is transforming the whole universe.' It is all one continuous movement for him." (pages 167–168)

- What would it mean for you to "stop circling the wagons around [your] own group"?
- Practically speaking, what would it look like in your own life to know that "all suffering is both *our suffering and God's suffering*"?

FOURTEEN

The Resurrection Journey

"'Everything will be all right in the end. If it's not all right, it is not yet the end.'"

—The Best Exotic Marigold Hotel (page 169)

1. Reflection

"I believe in 'a new heaven and a new earth' (Isaiah 65:17, Romans 8:18–25, 2 Peter 3:13, Revelation 21:1); and I believe *the resurrection of Jesus is like the icon you click on your computer to get to the right place.*

"Christianity's true and unique story line has always been incarnation. If creation is 'very good' (Genesis 1:34) at its very inception, how could such a divine agenda ever be undone by any human failure to fully cooperate? 'Very good' sets us on a trajectory toward resurrection, it seems to me." (page 172)

- How does the notion that *"Christianity's true and unique story line has always been incarnation"* sit with you?

- What is your experience of creation as "very good"?

2. Reflection

"Many Christians sadly prefer to read these passages from a world-view of scarcity instead of the Gospel of divine abundance, and this constant resistance to Infinite Love is revealed in the biblical text itself. The problem is tied up with the solution, as it were, the pushback included in the resolution. There seems to be a necessary villain in every story line, and the villain is almost always found inside the biblical text. I know no other way to make sense of the Bible's many obvious contradictions and inconsistencies about God.

"The ungenerous mind does not like the wedding banquet. It prefers a dualistic courtroom scene as its metaphor for the end of time, which is why Matthew 25's sheep and goats are the end-times parable that most people remember, even though they do not follow its actual message about care for the poor, and remember only the scary verdict at the end. In other words, Matthew 25:46b is allowed to trump all of Matthew 25:31–45. Scared people remember threats and do not hear invitations!" (page 173)

- Thinking of worldviews of "scarcity" or "divine abundance," which most characterizes your perspective?

Re-read the parable of the sheep and the goats in Matthew chapter 25.

- Does it read as more of a threat or more of an invitation?

- Journal what this parable evokes in you.

3. Reflection

"The great Athanasius (298–373) put it this way: *'God [in Christ] became the bearer of flesh [for a time] so that humanity could become the bearer of Spirit forever.'* This was the Great Exchange. Jesus was meant to be the guarantee that divinity can indeed reside within humanity, which is always our great doubt and denial. And once that is possible, then most of our problems are already solved. Resurrection of both persons and planets becomes a foregone conclusion! What that exactly means, of course, I cannot possibly know (1 Corinthians 2:9), but I can say:

"*Creation is the first and probably the final Bible, Incarnation is already Redemption, Christmas is already Easter, and Jesus is already Christ.*

"Simply put, if death is not possible for the Christ, then it is not possible for anything that 'shares in the divine nature' (2 Peter 1:4)." (page 179)

▸ Reflect on this quotation in the light of Fr. Richard's previous invitation "to linger with an idea, to focus on it until it engages your body, your heart, your awareness of the physical world around you, and most especially your core connection with a larger field." (page 8)

▸ Notice what resonates with you. Take some time to journal your experience.

4. Contemplative Sit

Leading in with the quotation below, practice a contemplative sit. You may wish to set a timer or digital prayer bell for 15, 20, or 25 minutes, so that you know when to finish.

Seat yourself in a quiet area. Once you are settled, read the passage aloud—this is the opening text for your sit:

> "'Resurrection' is another word for change, but particularly positive change—which we tend to see only in the long run. In the short run, it often just looks like death. The Preface to the Catholic funeral liturgy says, 'Life is not ended, it is merely changed.'" (pages 170–171)

‣ Notice any tightness in your shoulders and neck and allow any tension in your muscles to relax.

‣ Allow your back to rest in an aligned, neutral position.

‣ Ground yourself and allow your breathing to settle. Then read the following aloud, pausing between each sentence:

"I am not trying to 'achieve' anything. There are no goals. I am simply becoming aware of this moment. Becoming aware of my presence in this moment. As I notice any distractions, thoughts, judgments, decisions, ideas that cross my mind, I let them go for now, focusing instead on my moment-by-moment experience of being present to What Is. God's Presence. The Larger Field. *En Cristo.*

"As I become distracted, frustrated, or confused, I consciously return to offering my moment-by-moment presence to God's Presence. God's Presence is already within me, whether I'm aware of it or not. No offering up is needed—I am offering in. Into the silence. Into each moment that I sit in contemplation.

"'Life is not ended, it is merely changed.'" [Pause]

‣ Ring a prayer bell to indicate that the contemplative sit has begun.

Silence for 15, 20, or 25 minutes

Once the closing prayer bell or timer sounds, briefly write down what this experience was like for you.

5. Connection

> *"It will really help you, Christian or not, if you can begin to see Jesus—and Christ—as coming out of Reality, naming it, giving it a face, not appearing to Reality from another world.* There is no group to join here, no need to sign on the dotted line, only a generous moment of recognition that the Inner and the Outer are one and the same. Our inner meaning and Christ's outer meaning, if you will. They mirror one another: Human anthropology matches a divine theology. How is that for one Great Ecosystem? If one's theology (view of God) does not significantly change one's anthropology (view of humanity), it is largely what we call a 'head trip.'" (page 174)

- Engage in a creative activity that you often find relaxing. Choose something that usually makes you feel "connected" with nature, with yourself, or with the cosmos in general (e.g., taking a walk, engaging in a craft, cooking, writing, playing a sport, or anything else that both grounds and connects you in the moment).

- At some point during or after the activity, whenever you feel a sense of "flow" or connection, speak the following phrase out loud:

- "There is no group to join here, no need to sign on the dotted line, only a generous moment of recognition that the Inner and the Outer are one and the same."

- What emotions and sensations does this evoke? Note down any reflections you may have.

6. *Lectio* Practice

Read the following quotations a couple of times before moving on to the *Lectio* Practice:

> "'*Love could not bear that.*' On the whole, we have been slow to notice how God grows more and more *nonviolent* through the Scriptures—or even how this evolution becomes completely obvious in Jesus. Infinite love, mercy, and forgiveness are hard for the human mind to even imagine, so most people seem to need a notion of hell to maintain their logic of retribution, just punishment, and a just world, as they understand it. God does not need hell, but we sure seem to." (page 183)

> "*If you are frightened into God, it is never the true God that you meet. If you are loved into God, you meet a God worthy of both Jesus and Christ. How you get there is where you arrive.*" (page 181)

1.   With the first reading, allow yourself to *settle in* to the exercise and familiarize yourself with the words. Read the text out loud, very slowly and clearly. Pause for a breath or two before moving on.

2.   For the second reading, *listen* from a centered heart space and notice any word or phrase that stands out to you.

3.   After a few moments of silence, read the text a third time, *reflecting* on how this word or phrase is connected to your current life experience. Take a minute to linger over this word or phrase, "to focus on it until it engages your body, your heart, your awareness of the physical [and unseen] world around you." (page 8)

     You may want to speak a response aloud or write something in your journal.

4. For the final reading, *respond* with a prayer or expression of what you have experienced, inviting the infinite wisdom of God to support you in places of unknowing, confusion, desire, or hope.

    Allow the text to sink in and settle within your whole being before moving on.

7. Reflection

"People who are properly aligned with Love and Light will always see in good ways that are not obvious to the rest of us, and we still call that 'enlightenment.' Such folks do not need to 'prove' that Jesus is God, or Christ, or even perfect, as we see in the parents of the man born blind (John 9:18–23). They just need to look honestly at the evidence. Even the man born blind himself says, 'All I know is that I was blind and now I can see' (John 9:25). People of the Light will quite simply reveal a high level of seeing, both in depth and in breadth, which allows them to include more and more and exclude less and less." (page 178)

- ► Since reading this book and beginning this Companion Guide, how have you been able to see "in depth and in breadth"?
- ► Which people and circumstances have you been able to "include more and more"?
- ► How has this affected you?

8. Reflection

"The systems of this world are inherently argumentative, competitive, dualistic, based on a scarcity model of God, mercy, and grace. They confuse retribution—what is often little more than crass vengeance—with the biblically evolved notions of healing, forgiveness, and divine mercy." (page 183)

"God's justice makes things right at their very core, and divine love does not achieve its ends by mere punishment or retribution.

"Consider Habakkuk, whose short book develops with vivid messages of judgment only to pivot at the very end to his 'Great Nevertheless!' For three chapters, Habakkuk reams out the Jewish people, then at the close has God say in effect, *'But I will love you even more until you come back to me!'* We see the same in Ezekiel's story of the dry bones (Chapter 16) and in Jeremiah's key notion of the 'new covenant' (Chapter 31:31ff.). God always outdoes the Israelites' sin by loving them even more! This is God's restorative justice." (page 184)

- ▸ What could you do to bring this kind of healing, of "restorative justice," to your family, your place of work, or your community?

- ▸ If you were totally honest with yourself, what's *really* needed from you to *"make things right at their very core"*?

9. Reflection

"But now you have been told about the Eternal Christ, who never dies—and who never dies *in you*! Resurrection is about the whole of creation, it is about history, it is about every human who has ever been conceived, sinned, suffered, and died, every animal that has lived and died a tortured death, every element that has changed from solid, to liquid, to ether, over great expanses of time. It is about you and it is about me. It is about everything. The 'Christ journey' is indeed another name for every thing." (page 186)

In closing this chapter, take a few minutes to meditate on this passage, reading it as few or as many times as it takes for you to really connect with it.

You may or may not wish to journal your thoughts at the end.

Of most importance is that you allow yourself to simply be, without any agenda, as you meditate on the passage. Let the reality of the "Christ journey" sink in, in whatever way this moment finds you.

FIFTEEN

Two Witnesses to Jesus and Christ

1. Contemplative Sit

Leading in with the quotation below, practice a contemplative sit. You may wish to set a timer or digital prayer bell for 15, 20, or 25 minutes, so that you know when to finish.

Seat yourself in a quiet area. Once you are settled, read the passage aloud—this is the opening text for your sit:

> "Nonattachment (freedom from full or final loyalties to man-made domination systems) is the best way I know of protecting people from religious zealotry or any kind of antagonistic thinking or behavior. *There is nothing to be against, but just keep concentrating on the Big Thing you are for!*" (page 197)

- ▸ Notice any tightness in your shoulders and neck and allow any tension in your muscles to relax.
- ▸ Allow your back to rest in an aligned, neutral position.

- Ground yourself and allow your breathing to settle. Then read the following aloud, pausing between each sentence:

"I am not trying to 'achieve' anything. There are no goals. I am simply becoming aware of this moment. Becoming aware of my presence in this moment. As I notice any distractions, thoughts, judgments, decisions, ideas that cross my mind, I let them go for now, focusing instead on my moment-by-moment experience of being present to What Is. God's Presence. The Larger Field. *En Cristo.*

"As I become distracted, frustrated, or confused, I consciously return to offering my moment-by-moment presence to God's Presence. God's Presence is already within me, whether I'm aware of it or not. No offering up is needed—I am offering in. Into the silence. Into each moment that I sit in contemplation.

"Nonattachment . . . *There is nothing to be against, but just keep concentrating on the Big Thing you are for!*" [Pause]

- Ring a prayer bell to indicate that the contemplative sit has begun.

Silence for 15, 10, or 20 minutes

Once the closing prayer bell or timer sounds, briefly write down what this experience was like for you.

2. Reflection

Slowly read over these quotations several times, noticing the places to which your attention is drawn, and where you want to linger:

"Translations say 'she turned,' or 'she knew,' or 'turning to face him,' she cries out, 'Rabbuni!' which means 'Master' (John 20:13–16).

Instantly, Mary sees the one before her in a different way, you might say *relationally instead of merely physically*. She realizes it is still Jesus, but he has fully become the Christ." (page 191)

"I don't believe the resurrected Jesus was being aloof or rejecting Mary's friendship, nor was he afraid of intimacy. He was saying that the Christ is untouchable *in singular form* because he is omni-present *in all forms*—as we soon see as the 'gardener' at the tomb (John 20:15), as a wayfarer on the road to Emmaus (Luke 24:13), as a man tending a cooking fire by the side of a lake (John 21:4). . . . (I personally suspect this is the same kind of presence that so many people experience right after the passing of a friend, or shortly thereafter.)

"I believe that, by repeating 'my' and 'your' twice, the text is trying to communicate that the event under way describes one common and shared God experience—his and ours." (page 191)

"We used to know him primarily *by outer observation*, but now we know him primarily *by interior exchange*. (Which is how we all know Christ, and is commonly called 'prayer.')" (page 192)

Sit with the words and phrases that most resonate with you.

▸ How do they connect with your current life experience?

3. Reflection

"Unlike Mary Magdalene, the apostle Paul never knew Jesus in the flesh; he only and forever knew the Risen Christ. Earlier we recounted his experience of being struck down and blinded, and we moved from there to consider how his transcendent experi-ence—captured in his favorite phrase *'en Cristo'*—moved him away from narrow religion and into a universal vision. Here I want to focus on how Paul, in effect, started with Christ and rather quickly made a full identification with Jesus, whose *voice* he heard on the Damascus road (Acts 9:4)." (page 195)

"Jesus represents the personal and Christ the cultural, historical, and social levels. Paul really teaches both, although the second has been largely *under*emphasized until the last fifty years." (page 195)

- In what ways has your spiritual experience moved from being centered on the personal Jesus to being centered on a more universal, larger field?

- Have there been times when your spiritual experience went in the other direction, from being centered on a more universal, larger field to being centered on the personal Jesus?

Reflect on these experiences for a few moments, journaling any learnings and insights you may have, before moving on.

4. Reflection

"In recent centuries, Christians have largely read [Paul] as if he was focused on what it takes for individuals to 'go to heaven' and avoid hell. But Paul never once talks about our notion of hell! Most people fail to notice that. He would have agreed with Jesus, I think, that humans are punished *by* their sins more than *for* their sins. Goodness is its own reward, and evil is its own punishment— although the thought and language of that period led most people to ascribe final causality to God." (page 196)

- What do you understand by the terms "heaven" and "hell"?

- How do these understandings relate to the notion "that humans are punished *by* their sins more than *for* their sins"?

"Paul . . . was convinced that only corporate goodness could ever stand up to corporate evil—thus his emphasis on community building and 'church.'" (pages 196–197)

- Have you ever witnessed corporate goodness standing up to corporate evil? Describe what this was like. You may want to journal your response.

5. Reflection

"The first apostle was a woman. And saying that is not trying to be politically correct. It's true by the early definition of an apostle as a 'witness to the resurrection' (Acts 1:22).

"Like Mary, we must somehow hear our name pronounced, must hear ourselves being addressed and regarded by Love, before we can recognize this Christ in our midst. And like Mary, we usually need to start with the concrete encounter before we move to the universal experience available to all. Spiritual knowing is an inner encounter and a calm inner knowing that we usually identify with 'soul' knowledge." (page 192)

"Mary came to full spiritual knowing quickly because it was a *knowing through love relationship, and presence itself.* Notice that she knew and trusted Jesus's voice, even when she couldn't recognize him. How different that is from our more common empirical knowing, which limits itself to various kinds of 'proof,' to its own form of reason, and to occasional moments of specific divine revelation. I believe that if we don't learn how to send people on *inner journeys or love journeys,* the whole religious project will continue to fall apart, because we have no living witnesses of a transformed life." (page 193)

- ‣ In what ways is your experience of going on an inner journey or a love journey similar to that of Mary Magdalene?
- ‣ How is this book (and Companion Guide) facilitating your ongoing inner journey?

6. *Lectio* **Practice**

Read the following quotations a couple of times before moving on to the *Lectio* Practice:

> "He was struck blind for three days (which often symbolizes a time of necessary transitioning to a new knowledge), and he had to be led into Damascus by the hand. During these three days Paul lived in what I call '*liminal space*,' betwixt and between worlds; he took no food or water from the 'old world' he was accustomed to, and began his transition to a 'new world' in Christ. His is a classic description of conversion, and it follows the typical progression *from self-love, to group love, to universal love.*" (page 195)

> "The fact that Paul didn't know Jesus in person makes him the perfect voice to name the Christ experience for all of us who come after him." (page 196)

1. With the first reading, allow yourself to *settle in* to the exercise and familiarize yourself with the words. Read the text out loud, very slowly and clearly. Pause for a breath or two before moving on.

2. For the second reading, *listen* from a centered heart space and notice any word or phrase that stands out to you.

3. After a few moments of silence, read the text a third time, *reflecting* on how this word or phrase is connected to your current life experience. Take a minute to linger over this word or phrase, "to focus on it until it engages your body, your heart, your awareness of the physical [and unseen] world around you." (page 8)

    You may want to speak a response aloud or write something in your journal.

4. For the final reading, *respond* with a prayer or expression of what you have experienced, inviting the infinite wisdom of God to support you in places of unknowing, confusion, desire, or hope.

    Allow the text to sink in and settle within your whole being before moving on.

7. Reflection

> "Paul is often called the 'founder of the church,' and ... he expected and hoped for so much from those first Christian communities. He was the proud parent of 'children' and exemplars, whom he wanted to show off to the pagans. This admittedly often makes him look didactic and moralistic, which many do not like. But remember, *the greater light you are, the greater shadow you cast*. And Paul is a huge light." (page 197)

▸ Without analyzing or overthinking, answer the following questions:

  ▷ Where does my light shine the brightest?

  ▷ Where is my shadow revealed?

8. Reflection

"If your Jesus remains too small, too sentimental (e.g., 'Jesus, my personal boyfriend'), or too bound by time and culture, you do not get very far at all. For Jesus to become Christ, he must surpass the bounds of space and time, ethnicity, nationality, class, and gender. Frankly, he must rise above any religion formed in his name that remains tribal, clannish, xenophobic, or exclusionary. Otherwise, he is not the 'Savior of the World' (John 4:42) at all. This is much of the problem of credibility that we are facing now all over this same world that he is still trying to save." (page 194)

"I would insist that the foundation of Jesus's social program is what I will call *non-idolatry, or the withdrawing of your enthrallment from all kingdoms except the Kingdom of God.*" (page 197)

"Nonattachment (freedom from full or final loyalties to man-made domination systems) is the best way I know of protecting people from religious zealotry or any kind of antagonistic thinking or behavior. *There is nothing to be against, but just keep concentrating on the Big Thing you are for!*" (page 197)

- Reading these quotations, what resonates with you? Why do you think that is the case?
- What doesn't sit so well with you? Why is this?

9. Reflection

"Krister Stendahl (1921–2008) writes that Paul hardly ever speaks of personal guilt, or personal and private salvation—we are just trained to hear him that way! Stendahl goes so far as to say that in the undisputed seven original letters of Paul, he does not speak of personal forgiveness as much as of God's blanket forgiveness of all sin and evil. Sin, salvation, and forgiveness are always corporate, social, and historical concepts for the Jewish prophets and for Paul. When you recognize this, it changes your entire reading of the Gospels.

"I do believe Paul was implicitly an evolutionary thinker, which he makes explicit in much of Romans 8. Real power is now available and false power has been exposed in Paul's thinking, and now *it is just a matter of time till false power falls apart.* I have witnessed much of this evolution of consciousness in my own small lifetime— toward nonviolence, inclusivity, mysticism, and ever more selfless love, as well as more correct naming of the shadow side of things. This is the gradual 'second coming of Christ.'" (pages 198–199)

Describe your experience of a developing consciousness and awareness:

▸ What are the most significant milestones in the evolution of your own consciousness, from your earliest memories to today?

▸ *Who* and *what* are you now including in your worldview that you didn't before?

▸ What ways of being or ways of seeing are you transcending?

Reflect on the following line:

"Sin, salvation, and forgiveness are always corporate, social, and historical concepts for the Jewish prophets and for Paul."

▸ What does it mean for sin, salvation, and forgiveness to be corporate, social, and historical?

Either now, or in the coming days, reread some of your favorite or most challenging Gospel accounts through this lens.

▸ How does this perspective "change your entire reading of the Gospels"?

10. Reflection

"Some new studies claim that if we look at the statistics, we will see that Christians are not leaving Christianity as much as they are realigning with groups that live Christian values in the world, instead of just gathering to again hear the readings, recite the creed, and sing songs on Sunday. In that sense, actual Christian behavior might just be growing more than we think.

"Remember, it is not the brand name that matters.

"It is that God's heart be made available and active on this earth." (page 201)

"I do encounter Christians who are living their values almost every day, and more and more are *just doing it* ('orthopraxy'), without all the hype about how right they are ('orthodoxy'). Training instead of teaching, as today's coaches often put it." (page 201)

"Just as the Universal Christ moved forward for billions of years without any name at all, so the Still-Evolving Christ continues to do the same." (page 201)

▸ What do you make of this movement from orthodoxy toward orthopraxy?

▸ What is your own experience of aligning "with groups that live Christian values in the world"?

▸ In what ways do you sense that you are a part of *"God's heart [being] made available and active on this earth"*?

SIXTEEN

Transformation and Contemplation

"If Christ represents the resurrected state, then Jesus represents the crucified/resurrecting path of getting there. If Christ is the source and goal, then Jesus is the path from that source toward the goal of divine unity with all things." (page 216)

1. Contemplative Sit

"If we've been kept from appreciating a cosmic notion of Christ up to now, it has not been because of bad will, ignorance, or obstinacy. . . . Only early Christianity, and many mystics along the way, tended to understand that contemplation is actually a different way of processing our experience—a radically different way of seeing—which most of us have to be taught." (page 203)

"The contemplative mind can see things in their depth and in their wholeness instead of just in parts. The binary mind, so good for rational thinking, finds itself totally out of its league in dealing with things like love, death, suffering, infinity, God, sexuality, or mystery in general. It just keeps limiting reality to two alternatives and thinks it is smart because it chooses one!" (page 205)

"This is where a contemplative way of knowing must come to the rescue and allow us to comprehend a cosmic notion of Christ and a nontribal notion of Jesus. It will also help us know that it was not just ill will that kept us from the Gospel, but actually *a lack of mindfulness* and capacity for presence (along with our cultural captivity to power, money, and war, of course)." (pages 204–205)

Take a moment to meditate on any aspect of the above quotations that stood out for you.

When you are ready, prepare for a contemplative sit.

You may wish to set a timer or digital prayer bell for 15, 20, or 25 minutes, so that you know when to finish.

Seat yourself in a quiet area.

- ▸ Notice any tightness in your shoulders and neck and allow any tension in your muscles to relax.
- ▸ Allow your back to rest in an aligned, neutral position.
- ▸ Ground yourself and allow your breathing to settle.
- ▸ Allow thoughts, feelings and sensations to arise, exist and then fall away while you keep your attention open and large, connecting to the larger field.
- ▸ Then slowly read the following text aloud from Psalm 46, pausing between each line:

"Be still and know that I am God.

Be still and know that I am.

Be still and know.

Be still.

Be."

Ring a prayer bell to indicate that the contemplative sit has begun.

Silence for 15, 20, or 25 minutes

Once the closing prayer bell or timer sounds, you may wish to briefly write down what this experience was like for you.

2. Reflection

"Buddhism . . . provides insights and principles that address the *how* of spiritual practice, with very little concern about *what* or *Who* is behind it all. That is its strength, and I am not sure why that should threaten any 'believer.' By contrast, Christians have spent centuries trying to define the *what* and *Who* of religion— and usually gave folks very little *how*, beyond quasi-'magical' transactions (Sacraments, moral behaviors, and handy Bible verses), which of themselves often seem to have little effect on *how* the human person actually lives, changes, or grows. These transactions often tend to keep people on cruise control rather than offer any genuinely new encounter or engagement." (pages 211–212)

"What many have begun to see is that you need to have a non-dualistic, non-angry, and nonargumentative mind to process the *really big issues* with any depth or honesty, and most of us have not been effectively taught how to do that in practice. We were largely taught *what* to believe instead of *how* to believe. We had faith *in* Jesus, often as if he were an idol, more than sharing the expansive faith *of* Jesus, which is always humble and patient (Matthew 11:25), and can be understood only by the humble and patient." (page 207)

Notice your reactions as you read about the *how* of Buddhism and the *what* or *Who* of Christianity.

- What resonated and where did you sense resistance?
- In what ways are you currently experiencing the expansive faith *of* Jesus?

3. Reflection

"*To be forced to choose between two presented options is never to see with depth, with subtlety, or with compassion.* In our Living School here in New Mexico we teach a methodology that we call our 'tricycle.' It moves forward on three wheels: *Experience, Scripture,* and *Tradition,* which must be allowed to regulate and balance one another. Very few Christians were given permission, or training, in riding all three wheels together, much less allowing experience to be the front wheel. We also *try to ride all three wheels in a 'rational' way,* knowing that if we give reason its own wheel, it will end up driving the whole car." (page 213)

- What is your first impression of this "tricycle" approach?

"If we give reason its own wheel, it will end up driving the whole car."

- ► Where have you balanced reason with experience?
- ► In what ways could you apply this balance to how you approach God?

4. *Lectio* Practice

> "Any healthy and 'true' religion is teaching you how to deal with suffering and how to deal with love. And if you allow this process with sincerity, you will soon recognize that it is actually love and suffering that are dealing with you." (page 207)

1. With the first reading, allow yourself to *settle in* to the exercise and familiarize yourself with the words. Read the text out loud, very slowly and clearly. Pause for a breath or two before moving on.

2. For the second reading, *listen* from a centered heart space and notice any word or phrase that stands out to you.

3. After a few moments of silence, read the text a third time, *reflecting* on how this word or phrase is connected to your current life experience. Take a minute to linger over this word or phrase, "to focus on it until it engages your body, your heart, your awareness of the physical [and unseen] world around you." (page 8)

. You may want to speak a response aloud or write something in your journal.

4. For the final reading, *respond* with a prayer or expression of what you have experienced, inviting the infinite wisdom of God to support you in places of unknowing, confusion, desire, or hope.

Allow the text to sink in and settle within your whole being before moving on.

5. Reflection

> "But in the Buddhist frame . . . suffering is seen as *the practical and real price for letting go of illusion, false desire, superiority, and separateness.* Suffering is also pointed out as the price we pay for *not* letting go, which might be an even better way to teach about suffering." (page 217)

> "Both Christianity and Buddhism are saying that *the* pattern of transformation, *the* pattern that connects, *the* life that Reality offers us is not death avoided, but always *death transformed.* In other words, the only trustworthy pattern of spiritual transformation is death *and* resurrection. . . . The real goal is to choose skillful and necessary suffering over what is usually just resented and projected suffering." (page 218)

Take a few moments to digest the above quotations.

▸ What is your reaction to the line, "the real goal is to choose skillful and necessary suffering over what is usually just resented and projected suffering"?

You may wish to journal your answer.

6. Reflection

> "Contemplation allows us to *see* things in their wholeness, and thus with respect (remember, *re-spect* means to see a second time)." (page 215)

"In her book *Joy Unspeakable*, Barbara Holmes shows us how the Black and slave experience led to a very different understanding of the contemplative mind. She calls it 'crisis contemplation.' . . . Barbara teaches how the Black experience of moaning together, singing spirituals that lead to intense inner awareness, participating in de facto liturgies of lamentation, and engaging in nonviolent resistance produced a qualitatively different—but profound—contemplative mind." (page 214)

"It is largely a matter of your inner goal and intention, and whatever quiets you in body, mind, and heart." (page 215)

▸ What quiets you in body, mind, and heart?

▸ How might this be linked for you with developing a contemplative mind?

7. Meditate

"In Contemplation 201, you begin to see there's a correlation between how you do anything and how you do everything else, which makes you take the moment in front of you much more seriously and respectfully. You catch yourself out of the corner of your eye, as it were, and your ego games are exposed and diminished.

"Such knowing does not contradict the rational, but it's much more holistic and inclusive. It goes where the rational mind cannot go, but then comes back to honor the rational too. In our Living School, we call this 'contemplative epistemology.' *Contemplation is really the change that changes everything—especially, first of all, the seer.*" (pages 215–216)

Take a few minutes to meditate on the phrase,

> *"Contemplation is really the change that changes everything—especially, first of all, the seer."*

If you wish, it might be helpful to journal what this evokes within you.

8. Connect

> *"'God comes to you disguised as your life,'* as my friend Paula D'Arcy says so well. Who would have thought? I was told it was about going to church.

> "Authentic Christianity is not so much a belief system as a life-and-death system that shows you how to give away your life, how to give away your love, and eventually how to give away your death. Basically, how to *give away*—and in doing so, to connect with the world, with all other creatures, and with God." (pages 212–213)

Take a moment to meditate on the phrase,

> "a life-and-death system that shows you how to give away your life, how to give away your love, and eventually how to give away your death."

> ▸ In what ways can/does this giving away connect you "with the world, with all other creatures, and with God"?

9. Reflection

> "[Ken Wilber] and I both trust the descending form of religion much more, and I think Jesus did too. Here the primary language

is unlearning, letting go, surrendering, serving others, and *not the language of self-development—which often lurks behind our popular notions of 'salvation.'*" (pages 216–217)

"All of us travelers, each in our own way, have to eventually learn about letting go of something smaller so something bigger can happen. But that's not a religion—it's highly visible truth. It is the Way Reality Works." (page 219)

▸ What are you letting go of and surrendering to today?

"Yes, I am saying:
That *the way things work* and Christ are one and the same.
This is not a religion to be either fervently joined or angrily rejected.
It is a train ride already in motion.
The tracks are visible everywhere.
You can be a willing and happy traveler,
Or not." (page 219)

▸ Where are the tracks visible for you, along this path of seeing the Christ in every one and every thing?

SEVENTEEN

Beyond Mere Theology: *Two Practices*
Epilogue
Afterword: *Love After Love*

1. Reflection

"Unless the awareness of the Christ Mystery *rewires* you on the physical, neurological, and cellular levels—unless you can actually see and experience it in a new way—this will remain another theory or ideology." (page 221)

"Until you know what your own *flow* feels like, you do not even know that there is such a thing. And you must also learn to recognize how *resistance* feels. Does it take the form of blame, anger, fear, avoidance, projection, denial, an urge to pretend? . . . To get out of your programming is a big part of what we mean by 'consciousness.'" (page 222)

"This is probably why so many resist contemplation to begin with. *Because it feels more like the shedding of thoughts in general than attaining new or good ones. It feels more like just letting go than accomplishing anything."* (page 222)

▸ What words would you use to describe "your own *flow*"?

▸ What words (from the list in this quote or otherwise) would you use to describe the feeling of resistance to flow?

▸ How would you describe your current state of awareness along this continuum of flow and resistance?

2. Simply That You Are

"Practice is standing in the flow, whereas theory and analysis observe the flow from a position of separation. Practice is looking out from yourself; analysis is looking back at yourself as if you were an object." (page 222)

Take some time to prepare yourself before you begin Practice I: Simply That You Are.

Read the text aloud, finding a rhythm and a pace that suits you:

"Simply That You Are

"First, 'take God at face value, as God is. Accept God's good graciousness, as you would a plain, simple soft compress when sick. Take hold of God and press God against your unhealthy self, just as you are.'

"Second, know how your mind and will play their games:

"'Stop analyzing yourself or God. You can do without wasting so much of your energy deciding if something is good or bad, grace given or temperament driven, divine or human.'

"Third, be encouraged:

"'Offer up your simple naked being to the joyful being of God, for you two are one in grace, although separate by nature.'

"And finally: 'Don't focus on what you are, but simply that you are! How hopelessly stupid would a person have to be if he or she could not realize that he or she simply is.'

"Hold the soft warm compress of these loving words against your bodily self, bypass the mind and even the affections of the heart, and forgo any analysis of what you are, or are not.

"'Simply that you are!'" (pages 224–225)

3. *Lectio* Practice

Read the following quotation a couple of times before moving on to the *Lectio* reflection:

"The human need for physical, embodied practices is not new. Across Christian history, the 'Sacraments,' as Orthodox and Catholics call them, have always been with us. Before the age of literacy emerged, in the sixteenth century, things like pilgrimage, prayer beads, body prostrations, bows and genuflections, 'blessing oneself' with the sign of the cross, statues, sprinkling things with holy water, theatrical plays and liturgies, incense and candles all allowed the soul to know itself through the outer world, which we have in this book dared to call 'Christ.' These outer images serve as mirrors of the Absolute, which can often bypass the mind.

Anything is a sacrament if it serves as a Shortcut to the Infinite, but it will always be hidden in something that is very finite." (page 223)

The text for the *Lectio* Practice is:

"Anything is a sacrament if it serves as a Shortcut to the Infinite, but it will always be hidden in something that is very finite."

1. With the first reading, allow yourself to *settle in* to the exercise and familiarize yourself with the words. Read the text out loud, very slowly and clearly. Pause for a breath or two before moving on.

2. For the second reading, *listen* from a centered heart space and notice any word or phrase that stands out to you.

3. After a few moments of silence, read the text a third time, *reflecting* on how this word or phrase is connected to your current life experience. Take a minute to linger over this word or phrase, "to focus on it until it engages your body, your heart, your awareness of the physical [and unseen] world around you." (page 8)

    You may want to speak a response aloud or write something in your journal.

4. For the final reading, *respond* with a prayer or expression of what you have experienced, inviting the infinite wisdom of God to support you in places of unknowing, confusion, desire, or hope.

    Allow the text to sink in and settle within your whole being before moving on.

4. Reflection

"In 1969 I was sent as a deacon to work at Acoma Pueblo, an ancient Native American community in western New Mexico. When I got there, I was amazed to discover that many Catholic practices had direct Native American counterparts. I saw altars in the middle of the mesas covered with bundles of prayer sticks. I noted how the people of Acoma Pueblo sprinkled corn pollen at funerals just as we did holy water, how what we were newly calling 'liturgical dance' was the norm for them on every feast day. I observed how mothers would show their children to silently wave the morning sunshine toward their faces, just as we learn to 'bless ourselves' with the sign of the cross, and how anointing people with smoldering sage was almost exactly what we did with incense at our Catholic High Masses. All these practices have one thing in common: they are *acted out, mimed, embodied* expressions of spirit. The soul remembers them at an almost preconscious level because they are lodged in our muscle memory and make a visual impact. The later forms of rational Protestantism had a hard time understanding this." (page 223)

▸ What practices that "are *acted out, mimed, embodied* expressions of spirit" do you find most beneficial?

Either now or in the days ahead, take the time to engage in this/these practices.

▸ What effect does this have on you?

You may wish to journal your response.

5. The Divine Mirror

> "The goal of this meditation is to rewire you—both in your mind and in your body—to see all things in God, and God in all things. I find that if you practice this kind of seeing regularly, it will soon become an entire way of life, in which the natural and physical world can work as a daily mirror for you, revealing parts of your-self that you might not know otherwise, revealing the deep patterns of things, and most of all, showing that what we say about the Christ is true: the outer world is a sacrament of God." (pages 225–226)

Read The Divine Mirror meditation (pages 226–229) slowly, in parts or as a whole. If you notice that a particular line is speaking to you at some depth, pause and reflect on it until the feeling passes. Don't mistake this sensation for your own thoughts or mere brain chemistry. Instead, receive it as the flow of Divine Love.

6. Love After Love

> *"Our unveiled gaze receives and reflects the brightness of God until we are gradually turned into the image that we reflect.*
> —2 Corinthians 3:18" (page 233)

> "I hope this book has helped you to experience—and to *know*—that the Christ, you, and every 'stranger' are all the same gazing." (page 234)

Read the closing poem and notice what it evokes in you:

"Love After Love

The time will come
when, with elation,
you will greet yourself arriving
at your own door, in your own mirror,
and each will smile at the other's welcome,

and say, sit here. Eat.
You will love again the stranger who was your self.
Give wine. Give bread. Give back your heart
to itself, to the stranger who has loved you

all your life, whom you ignored
for another, who knows you by heart.
Take down the love letters from the bookshelf,

the photographs, the desperate notes,
peel your own image from the mirror.
Sit. Feast on your life." (page 234)

The Four Worldviews

"Your worldview is not what you look at. It is what you *look out from or look through*." (page 237)

1. Reflection

Read the following extended quotations and reflect on your experience of The Four Worldviews:

> "I have concluded that there are four basic worldviews, though they might be expressed in many ways and are not necessarily completely separate. . . . There are good things about all four of them, and none of them is completely wrong or completely right, but one of them is by far the most helpful.

> "Those who hold the *material worldview* believe that the outer, visible universe is the ultimate and 'real' world. People of this worldview have given us science, engineering, medicine, and much of what we now call 'civilization.' . . . A material worldview tends to

create highly consumer-oriented and competitive cultures, which are often preoccupied with scarcity, since material goods are always limited.

"The *spiritual worldview* characterizes many forms of religion and some idealistic philosophies that recognize the primacy and finality of spirit, consciousness, the invisible world behind all manifestations. It can be seen in Platonic thought; various forms of Gnosticism . . . ; some schools of psychology; in the forms of spirituality called 'esoteric' or 'New Age'; and in the many interior-focused or spiritualized forms of all religions, including much of Christianity. This worldview is partially good too, because it maintains the reality of the spiritual world, which many materialists deny. But taken too far it can become ethereal and disembodied, disregarding ordinary human needs and denying the need for good psychology, anthropology, or societal issues of peace and justice. . . .

"Those holding what I call the *priestly worldview* are generally sophisticated, trained, and experienced people and traditions that feel their job is to help us put matter and Spirit together. They are the holders of the law, the scriptures, and the rituals; they include gurus, ministers, therapists, and sacred communities. People of the priestly worldview help us make good connections that are not always obvious between the material and spiritual worlds. But the downside is that this view assumes that the two worlds are actually separate and need someone to bind them back together (which is the meaning of the word 'religion': *re-ligio*, or *re-ligament*, and also the root meaning of the term *'yoga'*). . . . It describes what most of us think of as organized religion and much of the self-help world . . . and its 'priests' vary from excellent mediators to mere charlatans.

"In contrast to these three is the *incarnational worldview*, in which matter and Spirit are understood to have never been separate.

Matter and spirit reveal and manifest each other. *This view relies more on awakening than joining, more on seeing than obeying, more on growth in consciousness and love than on clergy, experts, morality, scriptures, or rituals. The code word I am using in this entire book for this worldview is simply 'Christ.'* Those who fight this worldview the most tend to be adherents of the other three, but for three different reasons.

"In Christian history, we see the *incarnational worldview* most strongly in the early Eastern Fathers, Celtic spirituality, many mystics who combined prayer with intense social involvement, Franciscanism in general, many nature mystics, and contemporary eco-spirituality. In general, the *materialistic worldview* is held in the technocratic world and areas its adherents colonize; the *spiritual worldview* is held by the whole spectrum of heady and esoteric people; and the *priestly worldview* is almost all of organized religion." (pages 237–240)

▸ Which of these four was your dominant worldview during your formative years?

▸ Within which of the four worldviews do you most often reside today?

▸ In what ways is your worldview evolving?

▸ How has reading *The Universal Christ* shaped your worldview?

2. Reflection

"Each of the four worldviews holds a piece of the cosmic puzzle of reality. . . . When one too quickly and smartly says, 'All things are sacred' or 'God is everywhere,' that doesn't necessarily mean one has really *longed and made space for* this awareness, nor really integrated such an amazing realization. This is why we must balance Christ Consciousness with the embodied Jesus." (page 240)

"The incarnational worldview grounds Christian holiness in objective and ontological reality instead of just moral behavior. This is its big payoff. Yet, this is the important leap that most have not yet made. Those who have can feel as holy in a hospital bed or a tavern as in a chapel. They can see Christ in the disfigured and broken as much as in the so-called perfect or attractive. They can love and forgive themselves and all imperfect things, because all carry the *Imago Dei* equally, even if not perfectly. Incarnational Christ Consciousness will normally move toward direct social, practical, and immediate implications." (page 240)

▸ How do you relate to the *incarnational worldview* and the idea of feeling "as holy in a hospital bed or a tavern as in a chapel"?

▸ In what ways is your worldview moving you "toward direct social, practical, and immediate" actions?

▸ In what ways might you be resisting this social and practical dimension? What's really going on here for you?

3. Contemplative Sit

Take a moment to meditate on any aspect of the quotations above that stood out for you.

When you are ready, prepare for a contemplative sit.

You may wish to set a timer or digital prayer bell for 15, 20, or 25 minutes, so that you know when to finish.

Seat yourself in a quiet area.

▸ Notice any tightness in your shoulders and neck and allow any tension in your muscles to relax.

- Allow your back to rest in an aligned, neutral position.

- Ground yourself and allow your breathing to settle.

- Allow thoughts, feelings and sensations to arise, exist and then fall away while you keep your attention open and large, connecting to the larger field.

- Then slowly read the following text aloud from Psalm 46, pausing between each line:

"Be still and know that I am God.

Be still and know that I am.

Be still and know.

Be still.

Be."

Ring a prayer bell to indicate that the contemplative sit has begun.

Silence for 15, 20, or 25 minutes

Once the closing prayer bell or timer sounds, you may wish to briefly write down what this experience was like for you.

4. *Lectio* Practice

Read this quotation a couple of times before moving on to the *Lectio* reflection:

"As I have studied the two-thousand-year history of Christianity, I've noticed how most of our historic fights and divisions were about power or semantics: Who holds the symbols or has the right to present the symbols? Who is using the right words? Who is following the often arbitrary church protocols based on Scriptures? How does one do the rituals properly? and other nonessentials. (This will always happen when you do not know the essentials.) And all of this substituting for—yet surely longing for—in-depth experience of God or the Infinite." (pages 240–241)

The text for the *Lectio* Practice is:

"This . . . in-depth experience of God or the Infinite."

1. With the first reading, allow yourself to *settle in* to the exercise and familiarize yourself with the words. Read the text out loud, very slowly and clearly. Pause for a breath or two before moving on.

2. For the second reading, *listen* from a centered heart space and notice any word or phrase that stands out to you.

3. After a few moments of silence, read the text a third time, *reflecting* on how this word or phrase is connected to your current life experience. Take a minute to linger over this word or phrase, "to focus on it until it engages your body, your heart, your awareness of the physical [and unseen] world around you." (page 8)

   You may want to speak a response aloud or write something in your journal.

4. For the final reading, *respond* with a prayer or expression of what you have experienced, inviting the infinite wisdom of God to support you in places of unknowing, confusion, desire, or hope.

Allow the text to sink in and settle within your whole being before concluding.

The Pattern of Spiritual Transformation

1. Reflection

> "Even inside an incarnational worldview, we grow by passing beyond some perfect order, through a usually painful and seemingly unnecessary disorder, to an enlightened reorder or 'resurrection.' This is the 'pattern that connects' and solidifies our relationship with everything around us. . . . We could point to the classic 'Hero's Journey' charted by Joseph Campbell; the Four Seasons or Four Directions of most Native religions; the epic accounts of exodus, exile, and Promised Land of the Jewish people, followed by the cross, death, and resurrection narrative of Christianity." (page 243)

> "We must be moved from *Order* to *Disorder* and then ultimately to *Reorder*." (page 244)

▸ What resonates with you as you read about this Hero's Journey, this moving from *Order* to *Disorder* to *Reorder*?

2. Reflection

"ORDER: At this first stage, *if we are granted it (and not all are)*, we feel innocent and safe. . . .

"Those who try to stay in this first satisfying explanation of how things are and should be will tend to refuse and avoid any confusion, conflict, inconsistencies, suffering, or darkness. They do not like disorder in any form. . . .

"Permanent residence in this stage tends to create either willingly naïve people or control freaks, and very often a combination of both. I have found it invariably operates from a worldview of scarcity and hardly ever from abundance." (page 244)

- ▸ Did you experience an initial period of innocence and safety in life? If you did, what was that like?

- ▸ If you did not experience it at the outset, have you had moments or glimpses of it since? If so, recall a particular memory and describe what that experience was like in your journal.

3. Contemplative Sit

DISORDER: "As Leonard Cohen puts it, 'There is a crack in everything, that's how the light gets in.' . . . This is the disorder stage, or what we call from the Adam and Eve story the 'fall.' It is *necessary in some form* if any real growth is to occur; but some of us find this stage so uncomfortable we try to flee back to our first created order—even if it is killing us. Others today seem to have given up and decided that 'there is no universal order,' or at least no order we will submit to. . . .

"Permanent residence in this stage tends to make people rather negative and cynical, usually angry, and quite opinionated and dogmatic about one form of political correctness or another, as they search for some solid ground. Some accuse religious people of being overly dogmatic, yet this stymied position worships disorder itself as though it were a dogma: 'I reject all universal explanations except one—there are no universal explanations!' it seems to be saying. Such universal cynicism and skepticism become their universal explanation, their operative religion, and also their greatest vulnerability." (pages 244–245)

▸ Take a moment to meditate on any aspect of the above quotations that stood out for you.

When you are ready, prepare for a contemplative sit.

You may wish to set a timer or digital prayer bell for 15, 20, or 25 minutes, so that you know when to finish.

Seat yourself in a quiet area. Once you are settled, read this opening text for your sit:

"There is a crack in everything, that's how the light gets in."

▸ Notice any tightness in your shoulders and neck and allow any tension in your muscles to relax.

▸ Allow your back to rest in an aligned, neutral position.

▸ Ground yourself and allow your breathing to settle. Then slowly read the following text aloud from Psalm 46, pausing between each line:

"Be still and know that I am God.

Be still and know that I am.

Be still and know.

Be still.

Be."

Ring a prayer bell to indicate that the contemplative sit has begun.

Silence for 15, 20, or 25 minutes

Once the closing prayer bell or timer sounds, you may wish to briefly write down what this experience was like for you.

4. Reflection

"REORDER: Every religion, each in its own way, is talking about getting you to this reorder stage. Various systems would call it 'enlightenment,' 'exodus,' 'nirvana,' 'heaven,' 'salvation,' 'spring-time,' or even 'resurrection.' It is the life on the other side of death, the victory on the other side of failure, the joy on the other side of the pains of childbirth. It is an insistence on going *through—not under, over, or around....*

"To arrive there, we must endure, learn from, and include the disorder stage, transcending the first naïve order—*but also still including it!* It amounts to the best of the conservative and the best of the liberal positions." (pages 245–246)

- What is your impression of the quotations above?
- Can you locate yourself along a path of order, disorder, reorder?
- What are you rejecting or learning in your current phase of the journey?

5. Reflection

Read the following quotations and, going with your first reactions, journal what comes up for you:

> "Conservatives must let go of their illusion that they can order and control the world through religion, money, war, or politics. This is often their real security system. . . . True release of control to God will show itself as compassion and generosity, and less boundary keeping.

> "Liberals, however, must surrender their belief in permanent disorder, and their horror of all leadership, eldering, or authority, and find what was good, healthy, and deeply true about a foundational order. This will normally be experienced as a move toward humility and real community." (page 246)

- With which elements of conservatism and liberalism do you most resonate?
- What does this say about your (evolving) worldview?

6. *Lectio* Practice

> *"We all come to wisdom at the major price of both our innocence and our control."* (page 247)

1. With the first reading, allow yourself to *settle in* to the exercise and familiarize yourself with the words. Read the text out loud, very slowly and clearly. Pause for a breath or two before moving on.

2. For the second reading, *listen* from a centered heart space and notice any word or phrase that stands out to you.

3. After a few moments of silence, read the text a third time, *reflecting* on how this word or phrase is connected to your current life experience. Take a minute to linger over this word or phrase, "to focus on it until it engages your body, your heart, your awareness of the physical [and unseen] world around you." (page 8)

    You may want to speak a response aloud or write something in your journal.

4. For the final reading, *respond* with a prayer or expression of what you have experienced, inviting the infinite wisdom of God to support you in places of unknowing, confusion, desire, or hope.

    Allow the text to sink in and settle within your whole being before moving on.

7. Meditate

"I want to repeat that there is no nonstop flight from order to reorder, or from disorder to reorder, unless you dip back into what was good and helpful but also limited about most initial presentations of 'order' and even the tragedies of 'disorder' or wounding (otherwise you spend too much of your life rebelling, reacting, and suffocating). I'm not sure why God created the world that way, but I have to trust the universal myths and stories. Between beginning and end, the Great Stories inevitably reveal a conflict, a contradiction, a confusion, a fly in the ointment of our self-created paradise.

. . .

> "Maintaining our initial order is not of itself happiness. We must expect and wait for a 'second naïveté,' which is *given* more than it is created or engineered by us. Happiness is the spiritual outcome and result of full growth and maturity, and this is why I am calling it 'reorder.' You are taken to happiness—you cannot find your way there by willpower or cleverness." (page 247)

- ▸ In what ways have you "created or engineered" your spiritual experiences?
- ▸ In what ways have they simply been *given*?

As we draw this Companion Guide to a close, meditate on the following quotation until you feel ready to move on:

> **"We must expect and wait for a 'second naïveté,' which is** *given* **more than it is created or engineered by us."**

You are encouraged to write one final journal entry that brings some closure to the journey you have been on through Fr. Richard's book and this Companion Guide. Identify something you are grateful for as a result of reading this book.

Thank you for taking the time to work through this Companion Guide.

My hope is that this has been a formative experience for you along the contemplative path and that you will continue this journey, with us at the CAC, long into the future.

—Patrick Boland

SUPPLEMENTS
AND BIBLIOGRAPHY

Background to the Exercises in This Companion Guide

Guigo's *Ladder of Monks*

A helpful way of framing the contents of this Companion Guide is to examine an approach to spiritual practices that encompasses reading, meditation, prayer, and contemplation. *The Ladder of Monks* provides a helpful framework within which we can situate most of the practices contained in this Companion Guide.

Guigo II (1114–c.1193) was the ninth prior of the Grande Chartreuse Carthusian monastery in France. He outlined his approach to spiritual reading in a letter to his friend Gervius. This literary form, common in Medieval times, was "a carefully crafted exposition of the spiritual life."[1] It was written as an instructional text so that others could share, along with Guigo, the experience of an ever-deepening connection with God.

---

1 Finley, *Christian Meditation*, 75.

One day, while working with my hands, I was reflecting on man's spiritual exercises, and suddenly I realized that there are four degrees: reading, meditation, prayer and contemplation. This is the ladder that leads monks from earth to heaven. Although it has few steps, it is very high and incredibly long. Its base is set on the earth, and its summit reaches above the clouds to penetrate the heights of heaven. The names, order and use of these steps differ. However, when we carefully study their properties, functions and hierarchy, they soon seem short and easy, because of their usefulness and sweetness.[2]

The inference to the Genesis account of Jacob's Ladder is unmistakable. As Fr. Richard writes in *The Universal Christ*,

In Paul's story we find the archetypal spiritual pattern, wherein people move *from what they thought they always knew to what they now fully recognize.* The pattern reveals itself earlier in the Torah when Jacob "wakes from his sleep" on the rock at Bethel and says, in effect, "I found it, but it was here all the time! This is the very gate of heaven" (Genesis 28:16).[3]

The hope for this Companion Guide is that, as you move up and down this Ladder of Monks, your "awareness of the Christ Mystery *rewires* you on the physical, neurological, and cellular levels" so that you can "see and enjoy [the] Christian faith at this experiential level of awareness."[4]

2 Guigo II the Carthusian, *The Ladder of Monks*, trans. Pascale-Dominique Nau (San Sebastian, Spain: Lulu.com, 2013), 13.

3 Richard Rohr, *The Universal Christ: How a Forgotten Reality Can Change Everything We See, Hope For, and Believe* (New York: Convergent, 2018), 40.

4 Ibid., 221.

Lectio Divina

As mentioned in the Introduction to this Companion Guide, the Latin term *Lectio Divina* literally means a Divine Lesson. It refers to a practice of reading, meditating on, and praying with Scripture.

When the practice of *Lectio Divina* is referred to as "spiritual reading" or "sacred reading," it is taken to include both sacred texts and other spiritual writings, such as the lives of the saints, *The Cloud of Unknowing*, or Fr. Richard's book *The Universal Christ*.

Origins and Evolution of *Lectio Divina*

Briefly tracing the origin and evolution of *Lectio Divina* can be helpful to understand how to approach these exercises and why they feature so prominently, being included in each chapter of the Guide.

Jewish Tradition to Origen

The early Christian Church drew deeply from the Jewish tradition of reading aloud, meditating upon, and praying through Scripture. By the third century, as the spiritual practices of reading began to diverge from their Jewish origins, Origen of Alexandria (184–253) saw the study of Scripture as a sacrament and began to draw distinctions between the literal, moral, and spiritual meanings of a passage.[5]

Desert Mothers and Fathers

What we know as *Lectio Divina* began to emerge within the communities of the Desert Mothers and Fathers in the Egyptian desert. The first communities adopted Paul's line from Romans as their "rule for life": "Do not be conformed to this world but be transformed by the renewing of your minds" (Romans 12:2).[6] Pilgrims, therefore, journeyed to hear

---

5 M. Basil Pennington, *Lectio Divina: Renewing the Ancient Practice of Praying the Scriptures* (New York: Crossroad, 1998), 46.

6 Lawrence Freeman, Esther De Waal, Kallistos Ware, Shirley Du Boulay, Andrew Louth, and Others, *Journey to the Heart: Christian Contemplation through the Centuries*, ed. Kim Nataraja (London: Canterbury Press, 2011), 93.

a "word"[7] from these Ammas (Mothers) and Abbas (Fathers), such as St. Theodora and St. Antony, receiving a single word or a short passage from Scripture upon which to meditate. The hope was that this word (sometimes known as a Sacred Word) would raise their awareness, or consciousness (as Fr. Richard refers to it throughout *The Universal Christ*), thus deepening their connection with God. A Sacred Word, used as an aid to refocusing attention after a period of distraction, still features as part of the practice of a contemplative sit.

Monastic Approach
This form of *Lectio Divina*, deriving from the Desert Mothers and Fathers, developed over the centuries and evolved into what is now known as the Monastic approach. Here the focus is on listening to how God is speaking through a passage of Scripture. It begins by asking the Holy Spirit for guidance and discernment through the text. As one reads the text aloud, listens to it, and repeats it several times, they are trusting that the Holy Spirit will draw their attention to a particular word or phrase. Then they sit with this word or phrase and connect it to their daily life. They do not seek to "apply" it in any particular way, but simply to *listen* to it with an attitude of receptivity. When they have received this word with a degree of depth, they seek to rest in God's presence (in a contemplative manner) or to respond to God with thanksgiving for a particular insight, an expression of praise, or a declaration of love.[8]

Rule of St. Benedict
St. Benedict (c. 480–c. 547) gave sacred reading a central role within his famous sixth-century *Rule of St. Benedict*. His approach to reading included two to three hours of formal Scripture reading in the summer and up to five hours during the winter. As increasing numbers

---

7 Pennington, *Lectio Divina*, 46.
8 Thomas Keating, "The Classical Monastic Practice of Lectio Divina," *Contemplative Outreach*, October 4, 2008, https://contemplativeoutreach.org/classical-monastic-practice-lectio-divina.

of monasteries adopted the Benedictine Rule, these approaches to sacred reading became widespread throughout Europe. The practice of *meditatio* (meditation) saw monks repeat the words until they had memorized them. They would then engage in *oratio* (prayer) as a response to God's word.

The Introduction of Spaces[9]
Between the fifth and the tenth centuries, a huge innovation took place in how monks copied Scriptural texts: They began to put spaces between the words. When *scriptio continua* (continuous script) was read aloud, it would often sound like a constant mumble or chant. But once spaces were introduced, it became easier for the monks to spend time reflecting on more complicated Scriptural passages. Consequently, the solitary practice of silent reading became more commonplace. This new approach to reading facilitated a more introspective, interior spiritual practice.

Guigo II and the Scholastic Approach
As the Scholasticism[10] of the twelfth century developed, reading became a more intellectual pursuit. Over the following centuries, Scholasticism became increasingly prominent, eclipsing the more ancient way of reading Scripture. *Lectio* became associated with lectures and the academic world of the burgeoning European universities, where the focus was primarily on the exegesis of and commentary on Scripture.

Guigo II's approach to *Lectio Divina* was in the spirit of the Scholasticism of its time, and distinctly different from the more ancient and

---

9 I am grateful to Lee Staman, Library Director at the Center for Action and Contemplation, for his contributions to this section and information on the development of *Lectio Divina*.

10 The system of theology and philosophy taught in medieval European universities, based on Aristotelian logic and the writings of the early Church Fathers and having a strong emphasis on tradition and dogma. Oxford definition, *Lexico.com*, https://www.lexico.com/en/definition/scholasticism.

contemplative Monastic approach. It is much more structured and follows four distinct parts (which are described in more detail in Supplement II).

In general, the Scholastic approach to *Lectio Divina* begins with the reading of a passage of Scripture and the focusing on a particular word or phrase.

Lectio
This first step is called the *Lectio*, as this word or phrase is the "lesson" from God.

Meditatio
The second phase is to reflect or meditate (*Meditatio*) on this word or phrase.

Oratio
This is followed by a moment of prayer (*Oratio*), where, based on their reflections, the person spontaneously responds to God in "affective prayer."[11]

Contemplatio
The final phase is contemplation (*Contemplatio*), or a resting in the presence of God as the reflections and affective prayers subside and the person simply rests before moving on from the *Lectio Divina*.

This Scholastic approach is more structured and rational and usually excludes any emphasis on personal experience.

The Scholastic approach dominated for many centuries but, in time, *Lectio Divina* moved away from primarily focusing on the word and back to its Monastic approach of including the personal experience of the reader in relation to the word.

11 Keating, "Practice of Lectio Divina."

This Companion Guide seeks to combine both the structure and approach of the Scholastic approach with the personal, reflective experience of the Monastic approach.

The Cloud of Unknowing

One of the most famous spiritual texts ever written was the four-teenth-century *Cloud of Unknowing*. It was anonymously composed in English as an instructional guide to an unnamed friend, encouraging him to advance "beyond the active life to the highest contemplative life."[12] Much of its message was derived from aspects of the Monastic approach of *Lectio Divina*. Published during the rise of Scholasticism, around the time when the pope was silencing Meister Eckhart (1329) for his emphasis on "independent study, thinking, and experience,"[13] *The Cloud of Unknowing* emphasized "the value of inner, personal experience"[14] and, as such, was written in the spirit of the Monastic approach to *Lectio Divina*.

Decline of Lectio Divina

In the centuries that followed, the practice of the Monastic approach to *Lectio Divina* greatly declined. There were many individuals, such as Teresa of Ávila and John of the Cross, who drew deeply from this tradition that focused on personal experience. Overall, however, this experiential aspect of meditating on Scripture made way for the more Scholastic approach until that too diminished in importance and practice.

With the arrival of the printing press and the ensuing Reformation, even more emphasis was placed on the logical study of sacred Scripture. Over time, these more cognitive approaches to study became far more popular than the more holistic and experiential approaches

---

12 Anonymous, *The Cloud of Unknowing*, trans. Carmen Acevedo Butcher (Boulder, CO: Shambhala, 2009), 5.

13 Richard Rohr, "The Cloud of Unknowing, Part I," *Center for Action and Contemplation*, July 23, 2015, https://cac.org/the-cloud-of-unknowing-part-i-2015-07-23/.

14 Ibid.

upon which *Lectio Divina* is based. As a result of this increasing focus on "study," the practice of *Lectio Divina* faded into the background of spiritual practices for several centuries.

Resurgence
Only after Vatican II, in the 1960s, did this ancient practice receive renewed and widespread attention. Numerous books and articles have recently been published, from the 1970s onward, outlining the history and the practice of *Lectio Divina*.

Lectio Divina *in this Companion Guide*
The term Study Guide likely connotes a predominantly cognitive and intellectual approach to spiritual practice. For this reason, I have chosen to use the term Companion Guide and view it as an aid in reflecting upon our lives. Reading *The Universal Christ* and engaging with the *Lectio* Practices in this Companion Guide encourages us to delve deeper into our interior world, helping us to experience God with our whole body, mind, and awareness.

Overview of the Four Degrees of Guigo's *The Ladder of Monks*

The *Lectio* Practices in this Companion Guide draw deeply from the approach that Guigo II outlines in *The Ladder of Monks*. In the opening pages of his letter to his "Beloved Brother Gervius,"[1] Guigo gives the first of many analogies on the interconnected roles of the four rungs on the Ladder of Monks:

> The indescribable sweetness of the blessed life, is sought through *reading*, found in *meditation*, asked for in *prayer* and savored in *contemplation*. This is precisely what the Lord says: "Search, and you will find; knock, and the door will be opened for you" (Mt 7:7). Seek by reading, and you will find by meditating. Knock by praying, and you will enter by contemplating. I would like to say that reading brings the substantial food to the mouth; meditation grinds and chews it; prayer tastes it, and contemplation is the sweetness itself that delights and restores.[2]

---

1 Guigo, *The Ladder of Monks*, 11.
2 Ibid., 14–15.

1. Reading

"Reading is the attentive study of the Holy Scriptures by an applied mind."[3]

Guigo talks about reading as being "the basis [that] provides the material and leads you to meditation."[4] Although he was originally writing about sacred Scripture, this process can refer to a quality of reading through any spiritual work, such as *The Universal Christ*.

James Finley, reflecting on Guigo's understanding of reading, writes:

> If we look closely at the experience Guigo refers to as reading, we begin to realize that he is describing an experience that we ourselves have had. For each of us is no doubt familiar, at least to some degree, with the experience of being suddenly and interiorly touched by the beauty or depth of a passage of Scripture or some other spiritual work. It is just that we rarely read in the slow, attentive manner that invites these moments. And when these moments do occur, they tend to be so fleeting and subtle that we often do not realize the inner richness and full potential of what is happening.[5]

He goes on to say that, "There is no method here, no technique. For Guigo is encouraging us to read in a manner that is too sincere, heartfelt, and childlike to be reduced to any strategies of the ego whatsoever."[6]

3 Ibid., 13.
4 Ibid., 30.
5 Finley, *Christian Meditation*, 81.
6 Ibid., 82.

Reading in the Companion Guide

Lectio *Practice*

For each of the *Lectio* Practice exercises, the first of the four steps in each chapter is as follows:

> With the first reading, allow yourself to *settle in* to the exercise and familiarize yourself with the words. Read the text out loud, very slowly and clearly. Pause for a breath or two before moving on.

If you read through this guide in a quiet, solitary place, you might want to join with the early Christian practice of reading everything aloud as well. It's quite a different experience, one that can help us slow down and adopt a more reflective stance toward the text and toward ourselves.

2. Meditation

"Meditation is the careful investigation of a hidden truth with the help of the intelligence."[7] Also known in Christian literature as *discursive meditation*, this next rung of Guigo's Ladder "takes the food" of the word that has just been read and "grinds and chews it."[8]

The focus of meditation is to "get to the heart"[9] of the text. Guigo writes about how profoundly deep and meaningful a text can be, yet we can only access it if our "*heart* is pure."[10] As is the case with all spiritual practices, Guigo is referring to the preparation phase that is important before meditating upon a text. If we are distracted, if we are too busy or have many things swirling around our mind, it can

---

7 Guigo, *The Ladder of Monks*, 13.
8 Ibid., 15.
9 Ibid., 16.
10 Ibid.

be too difficult to step onto this next rung of the ladder. So, a time of quietening and self-examination can be helpful if we find the transition from reading to meditation to be too challenging.

James Finley has a lovely phrase for this *"meditative thinking,"* this personal reading of a text. He says that "we learn to ponder the thoughts that flow into our mind out of our childlike vulnerability to God."[11]

Once we are ready, we meditate by "taking a word into the depths of our sustained receptive openness, then allowing the word to resurface, intact and enriched by our own reflections upon it."[12]

Meditation in the Companion Guide

Reflection Exercises
Reflection Exercises feature more prominently than any other type of spiritual exercise in the Companion Guide. Given the confusion that sometimes exists in contemporary nomenclature, where the meaning of Meditation and Contemplation are often interchangeable, I have opted to use the term Reflection instead of Meditation. However, using the rubric of *The Ladder of Monks*, all the Reflection Exercises are essentially what Guigo would refer to as "Meditation."

Chapter 17: Two Practices
The two practices in Chapter 17 of *The Universal Christ* are also included in the Companion Guide. Simply That You Are and The Divine Mirror both draw deeply from the first and second rungs of *The Ladder of Monks*.

Both practices are designed to be read aloud, at a slow, deliberate pace. The intent is that we meditate on both of these practices so that they can lead us toward an experience of "embodied knowing."[13]

---

11 Finley, *Christian Meditation*, 88.
12 Ibid., 92.
13 Rohr, *The Universal Christ*, 224.

These practices have the capacity to lead us beyond the first two rungs, into experiences of Prayer and Contemplation.

Lectio *Practice*

The second step in each of the *Lectio* Practices reads,

> For the second reading, *listen* from a centered heart space and notice any word or phrase that stands out to you.

The quality of listening envisaged here is exactly that of Guigo's Meditation, involving a "prayerful introspection" where we "carefully [think] through the thoughts, memories, images, and connotations that come into our mind as we sit in the receptive openness of our reading."[14]

This naturally leads into the third step of the *Lectio* Practice, where you:

> After a few moments of silence, read the text a third time, *reflecting* on how this word or phrase is connected to your current life experience.

This next step into the text encourages you to:

> Take a minute to linger over this word or phrase, "to focus on it until it engages your body, your heart, your awareness of the physical [and unseen] world around you." (page 8)

Developing this kind of awareness naturally leads you into an attitude of prayer, the third rung of Guigo's *Ladder of Monks*.

---

14 Finley, *Christian Meditation*, 88.

3. Prayer

Guigo is clear, in this section of his letter to Gervius, that prayer is not to be isolated, to solely occupy the third rung of the ladder. Rather, it is to be present throughout the entire spiritual practice.

Sometimes, however, as we meditate on a passage, a fresh understanding or a new way of being can partially awaken something within us. It is at these times that we may consciously bring our confusion, our desire, our unknowing, or our hope to God in prayer.

Guigo writes that, "Prayer is the elevation of the heart towards God, so that it separates itself from evil and reaches toward what is good."[15] This essentially means that, in light of our reading and meditation, we have once more become aware of our deep desire for connection with God. The emotional energy of our desire for connection is conveyed through prayer, whether spoken, expressed in writing, or simply experienced as the silent embodiment of our longing for God.

Prayer in the Companion Guide

This emotional energy of prayer might build over a period of time, perhaps after answering several reflection questions, engaging in a few embodied practices, or simply as a result of going through several chapters of the Companion Guide.

At certain times, we may feel particularly moved to put down the Guide or our journal; to thank God for something; to ask God for comfort or clarity, for peace or for rest—whatever we sense to be most appropriate in the moment.

---

15 Guigo, *Ladder of Monks*, 14.

As we are aware of these interior movements and entrust ourselves to an ever-deepening connection with God, we may surprise ourselves with the emotion and expression of our prayer.

4. Contemplation

Contemplation is not something that we "attain" but something that is given to us, as a gift of grace. Whereas there was some degree of effort on the part of our ego in attaining the first three rungs of the ladder, now we find ourselves in a place of yearning "for an infinite union with the infinite."[16]

This is the culmination of all the other steps of Guigo's Ladder: "Contemplation is the elevation of the ravished soul in God, where it savors the joys of eternity."[17]

This rung of Guigo's Ladder is fundamentally different from the other three. It is something for which we can prepare but which we have no guarantee of attaining. As James Finley puts it,

> It is on this third rung of prayer's unconsummated longings that God unexpectedly does what God most loves to do. God bends down and unexpectedly places the fourth rung of the ladder firmly beneath our feet. Perplexed and bewildered, we gaze directly into God's eyes eternally gazing into ours. Everything is suddenly homecoming and communion. Everything is a love that comes rolling through, leaving in its wake nothing but love alone.[18]

At times, we will experience this momentary unity with the infinite

---

16 Finley, *Christian Meditation*, 98.
17 Guigo, *Ladder of Monks*, 14.
18 Finley, *Christian Meditation*, 98.

Divine, not as something *up there* but as Presence *right here*.

Seeking to engage in contemplation can often feel difficult, uncomfortable, and frustrating. Fr. Richard, in his book *Everything Belongs*, says that, "If the now has never been full or sufficient, we will always be grasping, even addictive or obsessive."[19]

Instead, when we contemplate and experience connection with Infinite Love, it can teach us to "know that things are okay as they are. This moment is as perfect as it can be. The saints called this the 'sacrament of the present moment.'"[20]

Contemplation in the Companion Guide

Lectio *Practice*

The final step of the *Lectio* Practice invites you to "*respond* with a prayer or expression of what you have experienced, inviting the infinite wisdom of God to support you in places of unknowing, confusion, desire, or hope." Although this is not contemplation *per se*, it is a doorway into what can become a contemplative experience.

It will be important, after "responding," to take some time to sit in open receptivity to God's presence. A moment of contemplation, as described by Guigo, can happen at any time, but we must be ready to receive it.

Contemplative Sit

An important line in the script for most contemplative sits reads:

> I consciously return to offering my moment-by-moment presence to God's Presence.... No offering up is needed—I am offering in.... Into the silence.... Into each moment that I sit in contemplation.

---

19 Richard Rohr, *Everything Belongs: The Gift of Contemplative Prayer* (New York: Crossroad, 2003), 61.

20 Ibid.

This really is, as Fr. Richard would say, "an inside job." The goal of the script for each contemplative sit is to help prepare us to be present to Presence. The reason we quieten our body and focus our attention on our breath or a sacred word is all to help us to simply *be*. "The contemplative secret is to learn to live in the now."[21]

The whole enterprise of each sit is to engage in a prolonged period of quietening. Thoughts and distractions will come and go, but as we gently return our attention to our moment-by-moment experience, we open ourselves up to the gift of God's Presence.

"Everything is suddenly homecoming and communion. Everything is a love that comes rolling through, leaving in its wake nothing but love alone."[22]

Aspects of Reflections and Other Exercises

The goal of each of the other exercises in this Companion Guide, from Nature to Imagination exercises, Presence to Reflection exercises, is to prepare us for moments of contemplation.

Some will find the body-based exercises most helpful, others the reflective exercises. Each can serve as a pathway toward deeper connection with God. Of most importance, regardless of the exercises with which we resonate, as Fr. Richard so succinctly puts it, is this:

"The contemplative secret is to learn to live in the now."[23]

---

21 Ibid., 60.
22 Finley, *Christian Meditation*, 98.
23 Rohr, *Everything Belongs*, 60.

BIBLIOGRAPHY

Anonymous. *The Cloud of Unknowing*. Translated by Carmen Acevedo Butcher. Boulder, CO: Shambhala, 2009.

Bianchi, Enzo. *Praying the Word: An Introduction to Lectio Divina*. Athens, OH: Cistercian Publications, 1998.

"Contemplation." Center for Action and Contemplation. https://cac.org/about-cac/contemplation/.

Finley, James. *Christian Meditation: Experiencing the Presence of God*. New York: HarperCollins, 2004.

Freeman, Lawrence, Esther De Waal, Kallistos Ware, Shirley Du Boulay, Andrew Louth, and Others. *Journey to the Heart: Christian Contemplation through the Centuries*. Edited by Kim Nataraja. London: Canterbury Press, 2011.

Guigo II the Carthusian. *The Ladder of Monks*. Translated by Pascale-Dominique Nau. San Sebastian, Spain: Lulu.com, 2013.

Keating, Thomas. "The Classical Monastic Practice of Lectio Divina." Contemplative Outreach, October 4, 2008. https://contemplativeoutreach.org/classical-monastic-practice-lectio-divina.

———. "The Difference Between Centering Prayer and Dom John Main's Christian Meditation." Contemplative Outreach, November 2017. https://www.contemplativeoutreach.org/article/difference-between-centering-prayer-and-dom-john-mains-christian-meditation.

Pennington, M. Basil. *Lectio Divina: Renewing the Ancient Practice of Praying the Scriptures*. New York: Crossroad, 1998.

Rohr, Richard. "The Cloud of Unknowing, Part I." Center for Action and Contemplation, July 23, 2015. https://cac.org/the-cloud-of-unknowing-part-i-2015-07-23/.

———. *Everything Belongs: The Gift of Contemplative Prayer*. New York: Crossroad, 2003.

———. *The Universal Christ: How a Forgotten Reality Can Change Everything We See, Hope For, and Believe*. New York: Convergent, 2018.

NOTES

Center for
Action and
Contemplation

A collision of opposites forms the cross of Christ.
One leads downward preferring the truth of the humble.
The other moves leftward against the grain.
But all are wrapped safely inside a hidden harmony:
One world, God's cosmos, a benevolent universe.